OD For the Intentional Practitioner

"Believe it or not it is easier to teach theory and concepts in organization development than practice, how to execute the ideas that make it all work. OD practices, of course, are based on theory but also on how one practices OD, and each one of us does it differently. You and I both may indeed practice OD effectively, but it will be according to different styles and behaviors of both of us. Kokkelenberg and Miller have provided a practice manual for both of us, an invaluable resource for 'how to do it', see for example, particularly Chapter 6, case 15, and Chapter 7. This book will be in your briefcase not your bookshelf. Many thanks, Larry and Regan for providing such a useful resource!"
—*W. Warner Burke, Ph.D., Professor Emeritus of Psychology and Education Teachers College, Columbia University.*

"Larry Kokkelenberg and Regan Miller have done it again! A thoughtful, straightforward, and caring welcome to the practice of OD. From the seasoned veteran to the beginning novice, OD for the Intentional Practitioner, is an absorbing read. For me, a seasoned veteran, it puts a lot of my divergent and often jumbled thoughts about OD into a meaningful perspective. For my beginning students, it is a clear and positive entryway to what can seem like an insurmountable practice to learn. A must read for all of us."

—Thomas G. Cummings, Professor of Management and Organization, Marshall School of Business, University of Southern California.

"Another great book by Larry Kokkelenberg and Regan Miller. For novices and experienced OD practitioners alike OD for the Intentional Practitioner provides a clear and engaging overview of this complex field, together with practical advice and insights drawn from years of consulting experience. wanting to help their organization to survive and thrive in today's Rich in useful case studies, exercises, and questions for self-reflection this book cuts through the jargon to provide a valuable tool for anyone in challenging times."

—Dr Linda Holbeche, Adjunct Professor, Imperial College, London.

"I am once again impressed with the way Larry and Regan bring a lot of information and experience into a coherent and easy-to-read book that demystifies and enlightens the subject and practice of OD."

—Glenda Hutchinson, Organization Development Consultant, IODA Co-Vice President of Conferences and Events.

"In this second book, Larry and Regan have added more basic, skillful needs for OD practitioners. We should be thankful for their work in adding these books to the many people who don't get enough practice attention in many education programs."

—David W. Jamieson, Ph.D., President, Jamieson Consulting Group, Inc.

"This is a wonderful resource that is well-targeted to individuals who sincerely want to be 'intentional OD practitioners.' The focus on understanding the organization as a system is spot-on. Also, emphasis on the practitioner's 'use of self' permeates the writing. Excellent use of cases and questions for reflection round out a well-written tool for internal and external practitioners."

—Roland Livingston, President Emeritus of the International Society for Organization Development and Change (ISODC).

"As a scholar who became an 'accidental practitioner' of OD several years ago, I thought that Larry and Regan could not top their previous book. However, they may have done exactly that with OD for the Intentional Practitioner. Once again, they write in a style that is clear, well-organized, and very thorough. The content is helpful and easily understood while at the same time thoughtful and profound. The most important element of this work in my mind is their emphasis on the central role of practice in developing skill and wisdom, or 'competence' as they characterize it. They correctly identify this as a shortcoming of much of OD higher education, and offer a variety of activities (cases, reflection questions, etc.) for readers to begin to overcome this practice gap. And once again, the return of the wisdom bits is much appreciated. This book should be required reading for all who engage in OD practice."

—Todd L. Matthews, Ph.D., Associate Professor and Department Chair, Department of Sociology, Criminology and Criminal Justice, Sacred Heart University.

"I have given Larry and Regan's book, 'OD for the Accidental Practitioner' to every consultant who has joined our firm and to clients. It is a masterpiece. And now, this book goes deeper into life as a practitioner and the thinking needed behind the actions we take. Another winner! Every practitioner and student of OD needs to have this book on their desktop or nightstand. Regan and Larry are helping to bring clarity and consistency to the field of OD, but more importantly to organization change."

—*Frederick A. Miller, CEO, The Kaleel Jamison Consulting Group, Inc. ODN Lifetime Achievement Award Recipient. Co-author: The Inclusion Breakthrough (2002).*

"Cases and questions, that's exactly what you'll find here. This book is full of juicy cases from the author's real-world work and consulting lives, each of which provides another view into the complex dynamics of the consulting relationship and the role that the OD practitioner can play. The questions are also very insightful and offer a compelling guide to what an OD person ought to be considering in the work. You won't find a recap of many OD theories here, but you will find a wealth of useful and applicable ideas for taking your OD work to the next level."

—*Matt Minahan, President, MM & Associate.*

"The book is not just a collection of theoretical frameworks; it's a practical guide that intertwines the science of psychology with the art of skillful practice in organizational settings. The insights offered are both enlightening and pragmatic, resonating deeply with the challenges and opportunities faced by both internal and external OD professionals.

'*OD for the Intentional Practitioner* ' is a must-read for anyone looking to enhance their professional journey in OD consulting. Its combination of theoretical depth, practical advice, and relatable storytelling makes it an invaluable resource. Whether you're just starting your career or are a seasoned professional, this book has much to offer. It's more than just a book; it's a companion for anyone committed to a career as an OD consultant."

—*Tom Mitchell, Ph.D. Associate Professor at the University of Baltimore.*

"Kokkelenberg and Miller's new professional resource, OD for the Intentional Practitioner, is an especially compelling example of double-loop learning, providing important answers to two key questions, i.e., what do we know? and how do we discover and organize what we know? Fortunately, the target audience for this volume, new and emerging OD professionals, will encounter a carefully articulated playbook that outlines the authors' theory-of-practice, a concrete and practical review of the assumptions, values, biases, and internal frameworks-for-action that they use to guide their choices and decisions in the moment. And so, by illustrating the necessity and power of careful reflection, they also make explicit what is most often tacit. That is, how do we actually learn what to do through experience? Using stories, questions, case examples, organization and systems lenses, practice scenarios, problems, solutions, and predictable uncertainties, the authors clearly show us both what mastery looks like and, even more importantly, how it develops. What we see, then, is a potent example of OD as an 'applied behavioral science.' This is a particularly important text for the reflective practitioner."

—Peter F. Norlin, Ph.D., Principal, Change Guides; Former Executive Director, OD Network.

"[OD for the Intentional Practitioner] is a useful book that provides readers/practitioners with insight that will aid them in successfully navigating a myriad of possible client needs and provide a roadmap of wisdom that may be applied in a multitude of organization scenarios. Your questions are a great launching pad to inspire the reader, again, to think more broadly. Not knowing the right questions to ask is what prevents the best solutions - your questions give the reader what they need to begin or move their process further along to a successful culmination…"

—Robert Stevens, Senior Organization Development Consultant, U.S. Office of Personnel Management.

"OD for the Intentional Practitioner is a book I would highly recommend to students, emerging practitioners, and seasoned OD & Change professionals. Kokkelenberg and Miller have provided an invaluable resource for both accidental and intentional OD practitioners—one that will serve as a functional handbook full of notes, highlights, and bookmarks rather than collecting dust between bookends. The content presents a clear and comprehensive composite of what have undoubtedly been the thoughts, ideas, and experiences of many practitioners. Intuitive and forthright, the book is filled with cases, exercises, and questions that provide direction and prompt reflection for the scholar practitioner in all of us."

—Anton Shufutinsky, Ph.D. , DSc, Chair, Organization Development and Change, Cabrini University, President, Changineering Global Vice Chair, Organization Development.

"Wow! Kokkelenberg and Miller have done it again. After their first book "OD for the Accidental Practitioner," they now provide a companion book for the intentional practitioner. From the big picture of *understanding organizations as systems*, to current cases on client issues, this book transitions beyond academic theory to practical insights for the intentional practitioner. This must-read OD book, as Kokkelenberg and Miller remind us that 'OD rarely follows a set of rules' and then they aid us in honing our skills with their timely cases, practical knowledge and their wisdom bits. Enjoy this resource once, and then keep it close for your next intervention – it's a fascinating read.

—Therese Yaeger, Ph.D., Benedictine.

OD

FOR THE

INTENTIONAL PRACTITIONER

A Book Written By Practitioners,
For Practitioners

LAWRENCE KOKKELENBERG, PHD

REGAN MILLER, MS

OD for the Intentional Practitioner:

A Book Written by Practitioners, for Practitioners

by Lawrence Kokkelenberg, PHD and Regan Miller, MS

ISBN-10: 7525269432

ISBN-13: 978-7525269433

Published by

7345 W SAND LAKE RD, STE 210 OFFICE 3266 ORLANDO, FL

689 219 883

www.parkerpublishers.com

Dedicated to

Mike, Logan, Mackie, Sara, and Chris

TABLE OF CONTENTS

INTRODUCTION

Why we wrote this book

At a conference, a recent graduate from a master's in organizational development (MSOD) program, said to us, "I do not know what to do next." They said they had all this knowledge but did not know what kind of job they wanted or how to put their recently acquired knowledge to use. They were not alone because we met many similar individuals. Additionally, over the last several years, when we asked OD consultants to illustrate the work they were mostly engaged in, we noticed that the majority would describe project work, or a specific task or project they were responsible for, i.e., executive coaching, leadership development, DEI program, etc. Seldom did we hear anyone say they were engaged in a large-scale organizational improvement initiative, a cultural change process, or really anything that reflected a whole system change.

While not a rigorous scientific survey, if this pattern is true, then the skills of OD consultants are being underutilized and organizations are not getting maximum value from the OD service provider (whether it be internal or external). Anyone in the organization can be assigned as the leader of a project, the responsible party. Using the OD consultant in this manner is akin to having a Ph.D. in statistical analysis teach 8th-grade math. Yes, it can be done, but does not use the talents and abilities of the individual very well.

In our first book, "OD for the Accidental Practitioner," we briefly introduced the topics of a skillful vs. a knowledgeable practitioner and the intentional vs. the accidental practitioner. We wanted this book to focus more on the intentional practitioner and improving their skills. We wanted to take a deeper dive into the practices of OD. We will leave the theory for academia and the researchers and theorists therein. Our goal is to increase the skillfulness of the OD consultant, be they accidental or intentional.

Becoming more skillful generally comes with experience, not necessarily with acquiring more knowledge, although knowledge is often the precursor to skill development. It is our goal that through reading this book, including examples, cases that are real-world situations, and through the encouraged discussions, readers will gain awareness, confidence, and the motivation to take on additional experiences and develop their skills as a consultant.

One way to move from knowledgeable to skillful and from accidental to intentional is to be curious about others' perspectives in practicing OD and decide what you will take and apply to your own practice. You may find that as you read this book, you disagree with our position or what we might be stating as best practice. This kind of curiosity and questioning is critical to moving into skillful OD practice and deciding how you will intentionally work in the field.

THE INTENTIONAL PRACTITIONER IN A CONFUSED FIELD

What attracts an individual to this career choice? In conversations with people throughout the country and with a brief survey of current OD consultants, several factors seem to frequently come up:

- People - working with people or helping them.
- System - working with the total organization, design, and development.
- Improvement - making the organization and/or people's lives better.

What attracts people to the profession is often reinforced and developed further in their education, but their responsibilities in the business world can be vastly different. This is in part because many organizations do not have a clear understanding of the capabilities within the OD profession. How is it that we have been publishing and teaching about the effects of the organization on human behavior for over 100 years (Frederick Taylor Principles of Scientific Management, 1909), and organizations, academia, the general public, and OD consultants alike do not have a clear understanding of the profession, a common professional association, a certification or a licensing process, or even agreement on what OD includes or excludes? In the drive to be all things to all people, the profession has become confusing to most people. The OD profession might do well to acknowledge that at minimum, we have contributed to, and quite possibly created this confusion. Just like any other organizational problem is rarely an accident, we have worked hard to get to this point. There are numerous contributions:

- The OD community has been very accepting of different definitions of OD.
- Many organizational interventions that might be better described as HR, project management, change

management, leadership development, coaching, and the like have been called OD.

- Different universities approach OD with significantly different curriculum leading to different beliefs about what OD is.
- Universities have placed their OD curriculum in different schools such as Business, Psychology, Education, and Sociology departments.
- Organizations have established OD departments or so-called OD departments that report to HR, Operations, Finance, Strategic planning, and other departments.
- The drive by the OD profession to be all-inclusive has contributed to being all confusing, there is a reluctance to exclude anyone doing almost anything and calling it OD.
- There is no certification, licensing, or educational requirement so anyone can call themselves an OD consultant.
- There are numerous professional associations, all with an OD division, each with a different focus and understanding of what OD is.

These and other reasons demonstrate that we have worked hard to get to this point.

Throughout time, various authors and scholars have used a variety of labels to describe the profession: organization design, organization effectiveness, organization structure, organization architecture, charting, organization development, organization improvement, healthy organizations, organizational strengthening, institution development, institutional improvement and many more. Not only has this confused the general population but also those in the field.

Story: Confusion about OD

We were chatting with an attendee at an OD conference and asked him how he came to be in OD. He told us that he was really in another area of the organization, but he really liked working with people. Eventually, he moved over to working mostly in the HR and Change Management fields. He said that senior leadership decided to create an OD department and because of his work with people, they thought he might be a good fit and asked him to be the director of this newly formed department. Additionally, they told him they were sending him to this conference to gain some ideas that might work in their organization. He was thankful for the opportunity, but said he really did not know anything about OD and asked his boss, "What is OD?" His boss replied, "I don't know either, that is why we are sending you to the conference."

He came to the conference and was absorbing everything he could. He said he was learning a lot and felt like a sponge just taking everything in. Although he was taking everything in, he was also confused. He still did not know what Organization Development was, and every time he asked someone, he got a different answer. He said no wonder why his company does not know what OD is, because no one else does either. He could easily associate some efforts with the same or similar efforts in HR or Change Management, but others he could not find a home for, like Six Sigma improvement efforts, social and community research programs, and zero-based emission programs for corporate America. He commented that everything seemed fragmented to him at this point with no clear path forward. He assumed that this would all become clear to him in time.

So, here was an individual who came to the conference to learn about Organization Development and likely left in a state of confusion. We often wondered how he would go back to his organization and explain to his boss what OD is, how he would form his own department, how he would tell others what OD is, and how or what he would contribute to his organization. Unfortunately, this was not the only individual we met who was either confused by the variety of offerings or by people claiming they do OD, yet they all seemed to do very different things. This encouraged us to write more about the field of OD and the use of self in this book.

At yet another conference, sitting with a group of graduating Ph.D. -level students, we were impressed with their knowledge of OD. They each had a clear picture of what OD was to them and it was uniform. This made sense because they were all from the same university. What took us by surprise though, was their naiveté about real-world corporate life, about how difficult sustainable organizational change really is, their lack of awareness of their own biases and preferences and how that affects their recommendations, and in general their lack of skillfulness. This prompted us to have discussions with others in the field, both academics and practitioners, about the current state of OD graduate programs, and opportunities in Academia. We thought long and hard about the contribution academia makes and can make which we have written about in Chapter 2.

Our goal is to help move practitioners to a greater level of skillfulness, and to encourage OD practitioners to have conversations about what the field is, and is not, and what it means to practice this craft. We have our beliefs and those are described and defined in this book, but the field will ultimately need a more solid foundation if we are all to grow collectively. We hope you enjoy what we present in this book, and it inspires you to action.

CHAPTER 1

Knowledgeable vs. Skillful

Knowledgeable: having or showing knowledge or intelligence (www.merriam-webster.com, accessed July 19, 2023).

Skillful: (1) possessed of or displaying skill: expert, (2) accomplished with skill (www.merriam-webster.com, accessed July 19, 2023).

In OD, practitioners often possess a wide variety of knowledge. Given the variety of careers where OD practitioners begin their journey, the knowledge is sometimes there without a practitioner even knowing. As we discussed in our introduction, how could someone who did not begin their career in OD transition into the field without any formal training? They demonstrated skills aligned with improving people and systems but were unaware of how these skills related to OD practices. On the other hand, some practitioners will spend a great amount of time pursuing formal education in this profession, either through universities, business courses, certification programs, etc. In all cases, practitioners can possess knowledge and varying levels of skillfulness.

One of the lengthiest, and sometimes difficult, transitions is to move from knowledgeable to skillful. According to Trotter (1986), their study suggests a five-step process for the development of expertise in any area. These stages are: 1) Novice, 2) Advanced Beginner, 3) Competence, 4) Proficient, and 5) Expert (Trotter, 1986, pp. 32-38). It generally takes ten to fifteen years to move from novice to expert (Huitt, 2006).

Fifteen years is quite a while to consider practitioners as emerging; however, when thinking about the complexity of OD, this seems apt. OD requires the ability to see a whole system functioning in real-time, deal with varying levels of emotions and complex behaviors occurring between small or large groups of people, and understand the many types of interventions that can be used to improve people and systems.

Obtaining knowledge and skills are not necessarily linear. There is a flow between the two and either one can be first. Acquiring knowledge involves learning, whereas developing skills involves active behavior. Knowledge can be obtained from many sources while becoming more skillful is generally limited to the experiences you have. One path to increased skillfulness is to expose yourself to as many experiences as possible, especially new experiences.

Developing skillfulness is a broad category and it may help to become specific in your quest for additional skills. Broadly, there are cognitive skills (decision-making, problem-solving), interpersonal skills (people), and professional skills (career). These areas are often broken down even further by various authors. Job responsibilities, organizational needs, and the evolving environment, including AI, hybrid workforces, and the gig economy, demand a diverse set of skills that OD consultants would benefit from learning and mastering as much as possible.

Reading this, or any book, will not make a practitioner skillful. The main goal of this book is to assist the reader in understanding how to move from having knowledge to putting it into use with clients. This chapter aims to reinforce the differences between knowledgeable and skillful and how to make the transition.

Knowledge is the state of knowing something while skill is the ability. Skill is the ability to artfully apply the information you possess to achieve results. Just because you know does not mean you can, and just because you can, does not mean you know. A consultant might know Kotter's Change Model - the '8 Steps to Change' (John Kotter, Leading Change, 1996), but that does not mean they are skilled at implementing these steps. Conversely, you might be good at helping organizations implement change but not know the Kotter model. One is not necessarily dependent on the other. However, the usual pathway to competence is to develop the knowledge first and then apply that knowledge to become skillful.

Knowledge can be obtained in many ways, such as reading, watching videos, attending webinars and podcasts, taking classes, participating in conferences, and talking with others. Developing skills, however, takes practice and opportunities must be present to practice. Becoming skillful can, and often does, take years to do. Further, it is not just the opportunity to practice, but the willingness and motivation to practice and to keep learning from each experience.

Group facilitation is a great example. The more you facilitate, the more you encounter unfamiliar situations, learn from them, and consequently, become more confident.

At some point, you realize that you are pretty good at facilitating all types of groups. Facilitation is one of the critical skills of OD because the intentional practitioner will frequently find themselves in meetings either as a leader of the meeting or a participant. Facilitating a meeting, especially without being assigned to lead it, demonstrates a tremendously helpful skill. Additionally, OD practitioners are regularly asked for feedback on meetings, such as their reflections on the outcome, the tenor of conversations and conflict, and other inputs related to group dynamics. As a result, an OD practitioner needs to learn how to observe a group and develop reflections in real-time. As a facilitator, this can help guide the group in their development. As a practitioner, this skill provides valuable data in terms of how a group is progressing and what actions may influence change.

OD is not a rigid science; a good practitioner rarely follows a rigid set of rules. There is an art and finesse to doing OD. There is a beautiful dance between the practitioner and the client, with the practitioner leading the way. This dance involves many roles including teaching the client, advising, partnering, observing, facilitating, encouraging, involving, visioning, monitoring, evaluating, and others. When to use each one is the dance. Who to dance with, when to dance, and what type of dance (foxtrot, tango, waltz, jitterbug) are also considerations the practitioner needs to make. This is where finesse comes in. For example, initially, the practitioner might respond to a client's request. Taking the client from the initial request to seeing the bigger picture and looking at the entire system to determine the root cause, working with the client to solve the problem, establishing infrastructure so that the work can continue after the practitioner leaves, helping the client create a vision for the future and establishing a strategic plan with the client while helping the client become more independent of your services, is often a long and complex dance. Knowledge alone will not get you there.

DEFINING AND MEASURING COMPETENCE

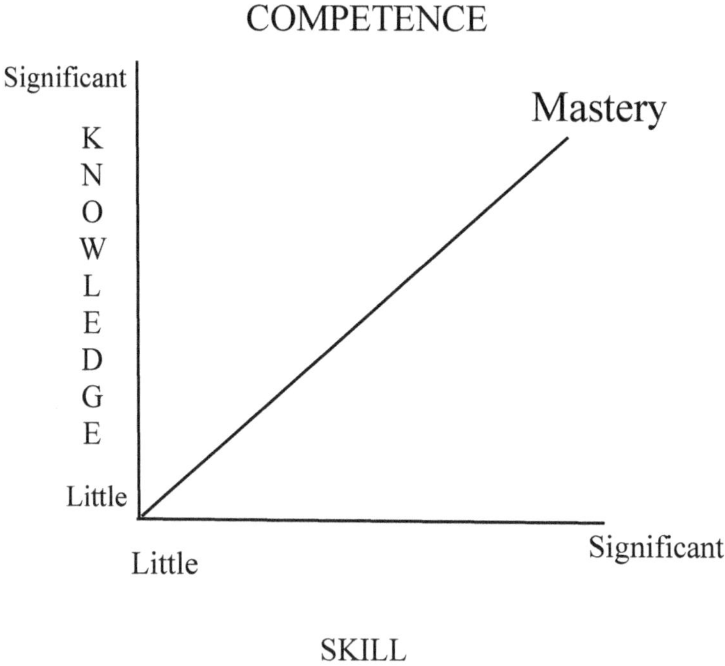

SKILLFUL VS. COMPETENT

A skill is defined as the ability to perform a task well, reflecting expertise in a particular area. Whereas competence encompasses having sufficient knowledge, skills, and experience—being adequate but not necessarily exceptional. A skill is more narrowly defined as having the necessary behaviors or abilities to perform an action, but a competency is more broadly defined as having the knowledge, skills, and abilities that enable an individual to be successful in their actions/endeavors and perform at or above required standards.

Becoming competent generally requires more time and energy than developing a skill; similarly, becoming skillful requires more time and energy than acquiring knowledge. Knowing does not make you skillful and having skills does not make you competent. Knowledge is information that is acquired, skills are behaviors that are exhibited, and competence is a proficient mindset, a confidence in self. Skillfulness and competence generally come with experience. Doing something repeatedly so that one can gain that experience is the only way skillfulness can be obtained. Experience does not come from reading books, including this one. You are unlikely to be an effective OD consultant with just knowledge, you need to be able to "do" OD, not just talk about it.

Various professional organizations have levels of competence such as[1]

---

[1] Adapted from 'Five Stages of Acquiring Expertise: Novice to Expert' at Rebecca West Burns' website https://www.rebeccawestburns.com/my-blog-3/notes/five-stages-of, accessed November 3, 2023.

- Novice
- Advanced Beginner
- Competent
- Proficient
- Expert

There are extensive descriptions of each category such as "Expert" has complete mastery of subject matter, can teach others, can perform skillfully with all clients/patients, can supervise the performance of others, and make improvement suggestions, etc. There are organizations that do not consider anyone with less than 10 years of experience to be in the higher categories. To grow through the categories, the OD practitioner must gain experience and apply knowledge, learning from both successes and mistakes.

Society and individuals only benefit when knowledge is applied. Knowledge tends to be broader based and theoretical while skills tend to be more focused and physical. Both are necessary for competence. Competence is sometimes further divided into specific and broad competencies. Specific competencies relate to particular tasks, while broad competencies are applicable to general or organizational requirements. For instance, skills in communication, time management, and conflict resolution are essential for everyone in an organization, whereas competence in a specific software program is required only for those who use it.

A continuum of development would be helpful in assessing competence. One such continuum might be:

Beginner	Little knowledge, little experience Some knowledge, little experience Significant knowledge, little experience
Intermediate	Little knowledge, some experience Some knowledge, some experience Significant knowledge, some experience
Experienced	Little knowledge, significant experience Some knowledge, significant experience Significant knowledge, significant Experience

If experience is the key to developing skillfulness, then creating opportunities in both organizations and academia for those opportunities to occur more frequently is the key to developing competence more quickly.

The following cases of Julian and Alana are examples of how self-awareness of the practitioner related to what they know vs. what they can do and can influence how client situations are approached.

Julian's Story

Julian was a certified project management professional (PMP), so he was brought in to help a group develop project management skills. Julian was also quite articulate and always well thought of by many of his colleagues. He was able to speak to almost any group, use their own terminology and influence them.

When Julian talked about project management, he would always tell you that it is not the charts that matter but the ability to lead a group of people to accomplish their goals despite all the obstacles. He would talk about project documentation, scope, timing, resources, and the like. He would give examples of project management models, charts, and steps in the process. Julian was knowledgeable.

When the time came to work with the group, Julian discovered he was facing many individuals resistant to the program that was being forced upon them. They were hostile, angry, aggressive, and confrontational. Julian never handled confrontation nor personal attacks very well and was unable to move the group off their anger and onto the project management coaching/training. It became a contest of wills and Julian was losing. Many people walked out of the program never to return; others complained to their bosses. Two complained to the HR department, two more went to their union representatives, and one person quit. The class was not a project management class at all, but a grievance and complaint session, where people were both verbally angry and close to being physically angry, shoving chairs around and standing closely in front of Julian's face. Julian was afraid, realizing he had lost control of the group.

This case illustrates understanding theory (being knowledgeable) without the skills for implementation (being skillful). Maybe of greater consequence is that Julian blamed the people, and their bosses, but never looked inward to see what his contribution to the problem was. By blaming others, he missed the opportunity to learn and grow for himself.

QUESTIONS

1. How would you fix this situation? Where would you start? What work would you do with the organization and what work would you do with Julian?
2. How do you handle passive-aggressive individuals?
3. How are emotionally intense situations handled in your organization?
4. How do you gain back control of a group once you have lost it?
5. Apparently, this group was not involved with any pre-training decision, what would you do with this group now?

Alana's Story

(yet another real-life example of an individual that was very knowledgeable but not very skillful)

Alana, a passionate and dedicated management consultant, showed immense care and compassion in her profession. She was also committed to continuous learning, often going to webinars and conferences. Quite articulate and filled with ideas, Alana would often cut people off while they were talking to jump in and give her ideas. She did so with absolutely no self or situational awareness to see that people were annoyed by her behavior. Even when the occasional person said, "I was not done talking yet," she would apologize and then do it again in the next 60 seconds.

There might be many areas Alana might explore including:

- *Self-awareness*
- *Sensitivity to others*
- *Situational awareness*
- *Listening skills*
- *Patience*

Whatever Alana might choose to explore, it is safe to say that this lack of communication or interpersonal skills will negatively impact her being a highly effective management consultant. Though knowledgeable, Alana lacked skillfulness. Despite her intelligence, her communication and self-awareness were notably deficient. Sensitive to others, no. Alana was more of a theoretician than a practitioner.

QUESTIONS

1. When others are not self-aware that their behavior negatively impacts others on the team or in the department, what is the typical way that is dealt with in your organization?
2. What is the difference between those individuals who have poor listening skills and those individuals who think they know more than others?
3. Who in your organization is not situationally aware?
4. Who is a poor listener? Why are they poor listeners?
5. What can you do to be a better listener?

ACADEMIA'S ROLE IN DEVELOPMENT

Academia offers education to its students. They impart knowledge and test to ensure understanding and retention. Generally, academia does an excellent job of giving students a strong knowledge base of OD, discussing theories of OD, history of OD, future of OD, Organizational Design, models of organizations, system theory, dialogic vs. diagnostic, DEI and social justice programs, green initiatives and more. As an example of how academia approaches knowledge development, listed below are core course requirements for a university in their master's program:

Core Courses	<ul><li>Social and Psychological perspectives in organizational leadership</li><li>Evidence based perspectives in organizational leadership</li><li>Advanced leadership assessments</li><li>Analyzing organizations</li><li>Qualitative data analysis in leadership research</li><li>Advanced multivariate data analysis</li></ul>
Elective Courses	<ul><li>Emotional Intelligence</li><li>Conflict resolution</li><li>Leading diverse teams</li><li>Intercultural leadership</li><li>Learning and development</li><li>Collaborative governance with nonprofits</li><li>Resource development</li><li>Community activism, leading social change</li></ul>

These courses provide comprehensive insights into organizational life. Undoubtedly, students in this program gain extensive knowledge about organizations. However, the program seemingly lacks any requirement or course designed for practical application of this knowledge, mentoring, and development of skills and competencies. Unfortunately, this may be the norm for many universities: graduating very knowledgeable people without a lot of skills or experience.

To enhance skillfulness and competence, individuals need less emphasis on lectures and PowerPoint presentations and more on practice, role plays, simulations, and hands-on implementation. It makes little sense to have incredibly knowledgeable individuals who lack opportunities to apply that knowledge and become more skillful. You cannot just read a book about bodybuilding and expect to have a better body, at some point, you must go to the gym and pay attention to your diet. Some universities may adopt a myopic view, believing their sole job is to educate and impart knowledge, whereas skill development is something the individual does after graduation, and it is left up to the graduate to figure out how.

Is academia graduating intelligent incompetents or is knowledge the necessary first step to developing competence? It is hard to think of someone as competent without having a good degree of knowledge; however, this is for the academics to decide. Academia could be an enormous help in developing skillfulness by designing programming for students that includes internships, job shadowing, applied classes, action learning, etc. This would be especially important for those intentional practitioners who go directly from undergraduate school to a graduate program. Learning the Thomas Kilmann model of conflict resolution (Thomas-Kilmann, 1974) in the safety of a classroom does not compare to facing an angry group of people wanting to know why you are there and what you can do for them or being in front of an angry union representative threatening grievances and work stoppages.

If you want to become skillful then you must do OD, not just talk about OD. The opportunities to gain experience may be limited. Students in OD programs may want to consider volunteering their services in smaller organizations that could benefit from OD support. Targeting organizations that do not have internal consultants or funds to hire external consultants may help create such volunteer opportunities. There is a need for systemic consulting in these smaller organizations and there are issues germane to smaller and family-run organizations that larger organizations do not have. Experience such as this would be invaluable for anyone entering the profession, and it would be a contribution to society. Academia can be an enormous help in matching students with experiential opportunities, as well as providing credit hours for students who take advantage of the opportunities.

Additionally, hiring the right faculty in the university programs is critical to designing education programs that address knowledge and skill equally. A best practice would be for prospective professors to demonstrate they have real-world application of their knowledge, to avoid those who can only teach theory. Many professors themselves may not have a lot of real-world experience, and if they do, it may be quite limited. Finding a professor who has significant real-world experience in a variety of organizations is a quality find because they can bring a practical view to their teaching. If we want better-prepared graduate practitioners, then it must start with academia and the types of individuals they hire to teach the students.

After reviewing many university job announcements for professors, we repeatedly came upon statements such as this: *"Applicants will be expected to engage in scholarly research and publications; teach at the undergraduate and graduate levels; advise undergraduate, master's, and Ph.D. students; serve on doctoral student committees; seek external grants; serve on department, college, and university committees; collaborate with the larger department, college, and university faculty groups; promote cross-program integration; and serve as faculty coordinator for the unit and lead the marketing and recruitment efforts."*

All these duties except one serve the university well but do not address developing students and prepare them for the work they will be doing after graduation. If we think of the students as customers and the university as an organization, then it appears that this organization prioritizes hiring people who benefit the organization. Yet, the only reason any organization exists is to serve their customers, because if there were no customers there would not be any need or relevance for the organization.

If the route many intentional practitioners take is through academia first, then academia is in a perfect position for developing both the knowledge and skills of the practitioner. Many students pick a particular university based on the reputation of that university in their chosen field. Also, many universities advertise a course being taught by a particular professor and the students sign up thinking they will have that professor, but then the course is mostly taught by a graduate student while the professor is off doing something else. In the commercial sector, it is called bait and switch. This poses a conundrum because the way a university develops a reputation is through professors who publish books and articles, make presentations at conferences, do groundbreaking research and market themselves and the university well.

The institutional pressure to publish or perish is a major organization (system) influence on academics who are teaching and love to teach. It is very difficult to serve three masters, teaching, researching, and publishing. Often, an academic cannot get tenure or achieve full professor status unless they are published. This is an example of the compensation, bonus, or promotional system influencing certain behaviors and not others. Naturally what suffers are those duties or responsibilities that are not rewarded (teaching). Good researchers do not necessarily make good teachers and similarly good teachers do not always make good researchers. Maybe these are two distinct specialties, educators and researchers, both need to be a part of an OD curriculum.

CONCLUSION

This chapter clarifies the distinctions between knowledge, skill, and competence, offering a pathway for progression across this continuum. We also expressed the critical role academia plays in developing knowledgeable, skillful, and competent practitioners. There is work to be done to ensure that intentional practitioners understand how to progress their skills through experience. **This book will not create skillful practitioners, but hopefully pushes readers to consider where they are on the spectrum and how to further their abilities.**

REFLECTION QUESTIONS

- Using the scale provided in the chapter, what are your levels of knowledge, skillfulness, and competence?
- Do you have gaps in specific areas where you need to focus?
- Have you reached a level of skillfulness or competence in any aspect of your practice? When? How did you know?
- How will you continue to grow along the spectrum? What activities will you engage in?
- What kind of opportunities exist for you to expand your experience?
- How many new opportunities did you take advantage of this year so far?

CHAPTER 2

Systems, Systems, Systems

System: A set of elements or parts that is coherently organized and interconnected in a pattern or structure that produces a characteristic set of behaviors, often classified as its "function" or "purpose." (Meadows, 2008).

SYSTEMS THINKING

Organizational models aim to help make sense of a complex system. Organizations have an unending combination of operating elements that are influencing and reinforcing their current state and it is critical to be able to identify and differentiate those elements to the greatest extent possible. OD practitioners excel when they are capable systems thinkers. Systems thinking can be defined as "a disciplined approach for examining problems more completely and accurately before acting." (thesystemsthinker.com, accessed July 19, 2023).

There are many resources, including websites, books, and courses on systems thinking, so there is no need to go deep into the principles, tools, and methods of systems thinking here. What is important is to understand that systems thinking is critical to successful OD practice and is a philosophy that can be applied to any organization. A systems thinking approach is necessary if an issue is chronic, has never been fully addressed, or seems to be complex and difficult to identify the root cause.

An OD practitioner can engage in systems thinking simply by encouraging an organization to focus on the "why" behind their actions. Why, how come, what for, and then what, are all powerful questions. Why ask for a training course on conflict management? Why is reorganization the best approach to improving performance? Why are new performance standards going to change the results? How come some teams get along and others do not? What results do we expect to come from this? Simply starting with this approach indicates that there is an issue to be explored more deeply. It also opens the mind to discovering what individual parts of the system are causing and/or reinforcing the current operations.

B.F. Skinner's theory of operant conditioning states that every human behavior elicits one of two responses: those that support (or tolerate) the behavior and those that extinguish it[2]. If dysfunctional behavior exists within an organization, some system or people, or both, must be supporting or enduring the dysfunction, or else it would have previously been extinguished. Dr. Deming proffered that 94 percent of variations in workers' performance levels are caused by the system, not by the individual themselves[3]. These are powerful formulations by a few of our past great social scientists. It certainly is an indication of how influential the system is on human behavior. For any

---

[2] Saul McLeod, Ph.D., "Operant Conditioning: What it is, How it works, and Examples," Simply Psychology, April 1, 2024, https://www.simplypsychology.org/operant-conditioning.html

[3] Hunter, John, "Appreciation for a System," The W. Edward Demming Institute, April 1, 2024, https://deming.org/appreciation-for-a-system/

behavioral symptom, there is likely something in the system that is in support of that behavior.

LONG TERM PROBLEMS

If a problem occurs, there is often a rush to solve it. While this is true sometimes, it is not true all the time. There are many times when organizational problems exist for years before being addressed. There are many reasons why this might occur including:

- The problem was deemed non-significant.
- The cost to solve the problem was more than the cost to endure it.
- Senior management was unaware of the problem.
- The extent or severity of the problem was unknown or hidden.
- There is a strong emotional attachment to the issue.
- Uncertainty as to how to address the problem.
- Whatever was tried in the past failed.

Anytime a problem has existed for a long period, it has become a part of the culture. Long-term problems are in some way supported by the systems and people of the organization. Continuing problems, at a minimum, are endured, tolerated, or allowed to exist whereas problems that are addressed are extinguished, solved, abolished, or at a minimum improved. Therefore, if there is a long-term problem, quick or simple solutions will generally not give the organization lasting results. It is necessary to explore the root cause and what supports the problem.

People are either unaware, enduring, or solving the problem. There are not many other choices. People that complain about the problem are in their own way a part of the problem. When a problem exists, it is the organization's problem, not just one person, team, or department. This, however, is not conventional wisdom. It is much easier to shift responsibility and say that the person, team, or department over there has the problem.

The intentional practitioner will encourage organizational ownership of all problems and thereby will build a collaborative team throughout the entire organization. Additionally, they will reduce blame and encourage ownership and proactivity. The intentional practitioner can anticipate that the resistance to change is higher in long-term problems than short-term or recent problems. Also, the stronger the emotions regarding the problem, the greater the resistance. Both issues can be diminished somewhat by having a broader ownership of the problem.

ORGANIZATIONS ARE SYSTEMS AND MODELS HELP DESCRIBE THEM

Organizations are living, interconnected ecosystems. Living simply means that it is constantly changing and not static. Interconnected means that every part of the organization is in some way connected or dependent on other parts of the organization. To think that a change in one person, team, or department does not have an impact on other parts of the organization/system is imperceptive. Large systems can overwhelm practitioners and clients trying to understand them. As a result, models are helpful tools to simplify the many different components of systems that can be assessed and redesigned.

There are many models identified in the literature; some have come and gone, while others seem to have withstood the test of time. Some models are better suited to certain industries and were often developed by individuals working within those industries. Some models are simple while others are very complex. Following Occam's razor principle, the simplest explanation is often the best. We favor simple models which we developed after looking at over fifty different models and in working with our clients. We provide two models here that we have used effectively with our clients and, more importantly, that have resonated with them as well. While simple to understand, they encompass the elements of most of the models we have reviewed. However, in the final analysis, a model is only a visual representation of a system, not reality—just as a map is not the road itself. **There is no one correct organization model, no one size fits all**. However, both of our models offer the practitioner a simple yet comprehensive outline for investigating the system.

MODEL 1

In the first model, there are three main areas/levers to consider and numerous subcategories within each main area. As with all models, some readers may like the simplicity, while others might encourage more categories for inclusion and review. Further, there is no correct order of priority, and the consultant might enter the system at any point and address what is most important and urgent for the client first. The phrase, "start anywhere, go everywhere" is quite appropriate when consulting with any client. There is also a fluidity that exists, and the norm is that work will go back and forth between the areas as the need arises. It is rarely, if ever, a once-and-done linear process.

The three main areas of focus are **culture, staff, and operations**. An example of what might be subcategories in each main area is listed below. This model is not rigid, and you might be working with a client that has other elements to consider and can easily be placed in one of the three main categories.

Culture

Every organization has a culture, and it is ubiquitous, yet you cannot see it. Culture affects everything the organization does; how employees relate to customers, how employees dress, speak, and interact, office layout, quality of products or services, reputation, etc. The following subcategories help to create a culture:

- Mission, vision, values
- History of the organization
- Leadership philosophy & style
- Policies and practices
- Politics
- Artifacts

Staff

Every organization has people who are affected by the organization and, in turn, affect the organization. An organization without people would merely be a legal entity, represented by documents filed in a court. Organizations do not exist without people. Further, no organization will ever change unless the people in it change. Organizations cannot change themselves; only people can instigate and implement change within organizations.

When contemplating staff there are many elements to consider including:

- Recruiting, hiring, onboarding, and retaining staff
- Employee engagement/motivation
- Interpersonal relationships
- Human capital management
- Training & development/continuous learning
- Work-life balance
- Level of collaboration, cooperation, teamwork, trust, conflict, and communications

Operations

The operations of any organization can be viewed as the output, with culture and staff serving as the input. Operational effectiveness can vary significantly not only among different organizations but also within the same organization, from one department to another. Why do competing companies, operating in the same geographical area, experience different levels of success, with one achieving high profits or a good reputation while another does not? Operational effectiveness is a tool/indicator of the level of dysfunction. This area encompasses numerous elements, including:

- Major systems, HR, Marketing & Sales, Administration, Production, Customer Service, Shipping and Distribution, Maintenance, Financial, etc.
- Physical structure, locations
- Alignment to mission/purpose
- Quality of products/services
- Organizational design/hierarchy
- Cost/efficiency of production or service

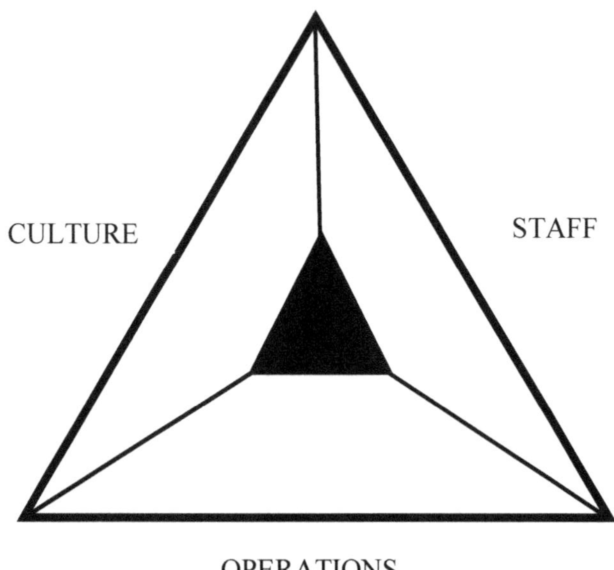

Most areas of organizational life can easily fit into one of these three categories, and many might even fit into two or all three of the categories. What is important is not where you put it, but if it is important to the organization, that it is addressed. After all, this is just a model, and the organization is important, not the model.

The above model is only dealing with the internal organization. There are many external circumstances that affect the organization as well as customer satisfaction. The OD consultant will recognize these external influences and factor them into their overall diagnostic and interventional activities.

All organizations exist to serve their customers and are sustained by them. Without customers, there is no need for the organization. This applies even in extreme cases. For instance, if every person obeyed every law, there would be no customers for the police departments, and there would be no need for jails, traffic enforcement, detectives, etc.

While Model 1 is primarily focused on the internal organization, there is also the recognition that other factors affect the total system which are identified in the schematic below.

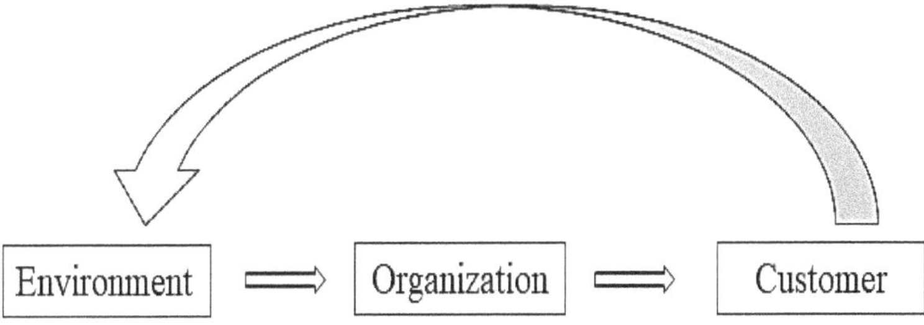

Model 2 considers the environmental conditions and since customers are external, they can be easily considered as a part of the external influences. It's also valid to integrate customers into discussions of organizational performance, as they are ultimately for whom the performance benefits. Once again, it is not where we put the topic that matters. If it is an important consideration, then what matters is that it gets put somewhere and is considered, investigated, discussed, and resolved. This leads us to Model 2.

MODEL 2

In this model, organizational life and its components are contained in the middle, and consideration is given to external forces that influence an organization, and the performance that results from these factors operating together. Just as with the previous model, a practitioner can start anywhere within the model and go anywhere. This is not intended to be a linear representation of an organization, rather it provides reasonable categories of the entire organizational system in which focused energy can be applied.

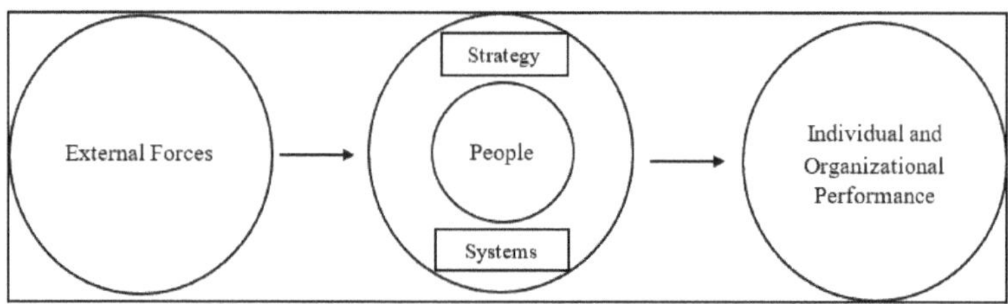

External Forces

Not all organizational operations are directly a result of internal decisions such as vision, strategic direction, people management, etc. Sometimes, external forces influence the adaptations an organization must make. For example, government organizations are regularly influenced by new laws or executive orders, private organizations might be affected by a natural disaster, social change, or any number of other factors. While these are not a direct result of decisions made by the leaders or people in an organization, they ultimately influence decisions within.

Strategy, Systems, and People

These factors are clearly within the control of the organization. Strategy is established by boards and leaders who set the tone, goals, and intention of operations. Systems are put in place by those who must execute the strategy and include governance, procedures, operational requirements, performance metrics, recruitment targets, staffing needs, etc. And people are the heart of the organization. Relationships and behaviors are indicators of culture and climate, levels of trust often determine production and performance, and leadership style/behavior greatly influences operations.

Individual and Organizational Performance

Performance is the output of the organization and can be measured at the individual and organizational levels. Performance can be a clear indicator of areas of success and limitations, if performance is low in an area, it is a strong indicator that some or several parts of the system are not operating optimally. When performance is strong, it is a good time to identify just what is working within the system to support this, and how to foster and retain these aspects of the organization.

Applying Model 2

The same as with Model 1, Model 2 is a way to conceptualize and simplify the complex organizations that OD practitioners are working within. Applying this model in a linear fashion is unlikely. As an engagement with an organization develops and progresses, you will likely move between different categories in this model and often will see where certain facets or challenges overlap across the model. Most importantly, the practitioner can use this, or any model to help define and manage an effort.

METHODS FOR PRACTICING OD

As is often the case, 'yesterday's solutions are today's problems.' Organizations are non-linear systems, rational thinking and logic do not always apply to cause and effect. **The time between cause and effect in some organizations can be years.** One policy, practice, or behavior may serve to produce a high-performing organization whereas another behavior that once produced high performance, now may degrade an organization's performance.

Understanding this concept is important to help open our minds to how an organization operates. As with models that can be applied to organization design and organization development, there are methods that a practitioner can apply to client situations. Methods are ways of practicing OD that give us some sense of structure and guidelines in our approach to understanding the system. Historically, most practitioners were aware of and/or applied process consulting methods and diagnostic methods. In recent history, there has been a rise in dialogic OD, with some practitioners stating they exclusively practice dialogic OD by applying its principles. Some practitioners are asserting that diagnostic OD is old hat, and the way forward requires deviating from this method and practicing dialogic OD.

It is likely more appropriate to assert that **all methods of practicing OD have their place and skillful practitioners can discern when and how to apply any method with a client.** To exclusively deviate from process or diagnostic OD means not necessarily identifying which elements of an organization's system are influencing the current operating behaviors. Failing to understand the history, and likely ignoring root causes, can easily lead to interventions that fail to help an organization adapt. However, strictly applying a diagnostic approach and failing to move towards intervention will only serve to perpetuate a client's challenges and never help make adaptations that may improve its operations. OD practitioners will increase their skillfulness by being familiar with the different methods and when to apply them. When determining preferred methods and applications, it is important to also consider the concepts with the use of self and identify which methods you work best with.

ORGANIZATION DESIGN AS AN APPROACH TO THE SYSTEM

Organization design is another systems approach to assessing and influencing the operating model. Often, organization design and development intersect and both fields can greatly assist in improving organizations. Organization design is often used as a synonym for organization structure, but this is false and limiting to the field. Organization design (as shown in many models for practicing this craft) uses a whole system approach to organization assessment and improvement. One of the most well-known models, Galbraith's Star Model™ (2001), encompasses several key elements: strategy, structure, processes, rewards, and people.

The differences between organization design and development are nuanced. We posit that the two approaches to organization improvement often go hand-in-hand. In fact, many organization design practitioners have also practiced organization development and vice versa. Why is this the case? Simply because of what has been described throughout this chapter, organizations are systems and there are many interconnected parts that influence their function, purpose, and performance.

Organization design more fully differentiates from organization development in its main objective, which is to design a way of operating that executes an organization's purpose and strategy most efficiently and successfully.

Organization design is best when it supports the purpose, mission, or strategy of the organization. There is no such thing as a perfect organization, nor perfect design.

Organizations in the same industry may legitimately have different designs because of their strategy. Adopting another organization's design in the same industry often does not work because of many internal differences, including physical structure, geographical location, number of employees, leadership style and personalities, different suppliers and environmental concerns, different culture, equipment, marketing, customer service, and sales philosophies, etc. Each organization benefits from a unique design that supports their unique mission and way of doing business and in that sense, there are likely no two designs that are exactly alike.

Using another organization's design, or an off-the-shelf design, eliminates the difficulty of developing a healthy structure, but the important process of discussion and designing the organization is absent, robbing the leadership of the input and creativity of everyone else who might be involved in the discussions. Participating in brainstorming and creative thinking about organizational structure consistently proves more valuable than adhering to any pre-defined model or design. The discussion involves everyone, helps everyone see the bigger picture and further helps all involved understand the reporting relationships, lines of authority, and communication and reduces resistance to change. When everyone is involved, it reduces unintended consequences, and generally, is more creative. Organization development may not always aim for large-scale changes but focuses on impactful, systemic improvements. In organization development, small changes can have large impacts while still focusing on the system. Organization development goes nicely with organization design in that its focus on the social and behavioral dynamics helps enable and reinforce the changes a design transformation is aimed at achieving.

THE PROBLEM WITH FOCUSING ON STRUCTURE

While organization design does not simply focus on structure, often designers are called upon to restructure or transform an organization by moving functions and job roles around. Restructuring is not a cure-all; it can sometimes introduce as many challenges as it resolves. A change in the organization design is often recommended when there are divestitures, mergers, acquisitions, international or rapid growth, financial losses, communication issues, unclear lines of authority and a whole host of other conditions. Using organization design to change an organization's structure as the sole method of problem-solving may be analogous to using a sledgehammer to pound down a nail. Yes, it may fix the problem but at what cost? Maybe all that was necessary was tweaks to the current design.

Rachel's Story

Rachel, an HR professional, was tasked with finding a consultancy to assist in reorganizing for improved performance and communication and to reduce employee complaints and unnecessary costs. A rather expensive firm was chosen. In their initial analysis, they recommended several solutions, including a significant change in reporting relationships, and lines of communications, physically moving several departments closer to each other and their mutual work, dissolving one rather problematic department, and breaking up the staff into several other departments, and management and leadership training.

Over two months of planning went into how they were going to implement all these recommendations and mid-level managers were brought into the planning sessions as well. Significant work was accomplished in laying out the plan, the time frame, and dealing with resistance to these changes. With one month left before they were to start implementation, the manager of the problematic department resigned, not liking the changes and the fact that he would no longer have people reporting to him. After this, the entire culture and atmosphere of the organization changed, so much so, that none of the other changes were deemed necessary or implemented. Over two months of planning by a significant number of employees and all that was necessary was a simple change of one person. Fixing the current system may be significantly easier than changing the current system.

Case Notes

This case underscores the critical need for accurate diagnostics before implementing organizational changes. The root cause was never established by the external consulting firm and instead, they appeared to be reacting to the many symptoms of the organization (a common practice) and then based their considerable recommendations on those symptoms. Quite frequently, a new organization design, a new organizational chart and new reporting relationships are the recommendations by external consulting firms and while there is usually decent justification for these actions, they may be expensive non-solutions. Consultancies often propose solutions without fully understanding the problem, emphasizing the need for thorough analysis.

This case also demonstrates the influence of one person on an entire team as well as the difficulty many organizations have with letting go of or removing non-performing or problematic managers and senior executives. In this case, there was significant time and resources wasted on planning, but at least no additional resources were wasted on implementation and the unintended consequences.

This is an example of using organization design as a solution to internal difficulties and while the solution may have worked, it would have been at significant cost financially, in personnel, and in unintended consequences, when a simple solution would have had equal effect. In the hard sciences there is often a single solution to a problem, but in the behavioral and social sciences there is rarely only a single solution to a problem.

Restructuring by itself does not improve performance, efficiencies, or enhance organizational capabilities. People will need to take advantage of the new structure and their behaviors will likely need to change as well. **The structure will influence behavior, not determine it.** It is natural for people to carry over to the new structure, their old behaviors/habits. Changing the structure without changing human behaviors is often an expensive mistake. Developing organizational improvements and enhanced performance is a time-consuming process and changing human behaviors, work routines, and attitudes is also a time-consuming process. Organizations that do well in redesign work tend to take time to involve all that will be affected by the changes, be creative, ask questions, brainstorm, anticipate problems, see the pros and cons of any decision they might make in advance of finalizing the changes. They approach the process systemically and patiently.

Organizational structures, policies, and practices that interfere with a mission add to the misalignment and dysfunction of an organization and make it difficult to perform well, while organizational structures, policies, and practices that support the mission and purpose of the organization enable high performance and help to distinguish the organization from all other competitors. The more dysfunctional the organization, the more misaligned it normally is and the more problematic as well.

FIX THE SYSTEM, NOT THE PROBLEM

Fix the system that caused or influenced the problem, not the symptom of the problem. Often when looking at a problem, we look at the individual(s) that are exhibiting (causing) the problem. While it could truly be a people problem, often, individuals were influenced or even encouraged by one or more elements of the system. For example, some companies have a need-to-know policy and then wonder why people are not communicating with one another. When you think systematically, you look for:

- What exactly is the problem?
- What factors encourage or allow this behavior to be present?
- What policies or practices encourage this behavior?

- How might our physical layout be contributing to the issue?
- Why does management tolerate this problem?
- How might management, consciously or unconsciously, encourage it?
- Is culture in any way influencing this behavior?
- What behavioral change do we wish to see and what can the system do to support those new behaviors?
- How is our organization design influencing the issue?
- What has been done in the past to address the issue and what were the results?
- Who or what else is being influenced by this problem?

It is a lot easier for people to change their behavior when the system strongly encourages those changes and a bit ridiculous to expect behavioral change when the system is supporting the old behaviors. The idea of the system influencing human behavior cannot be overstated. Humans have a marvelous ability to adapt to their environment and then reflect it to others. This reflection is often called the culture of the organization and is frequently a major clue to the system.

Whether you are an internal or external consultant to a client organization, you are a part of their system/culture. How does your presence and responsibilities affect the system? Not only are you a part of the system, but you are also impacting the system in one way or another. The larger the organization, the more complex the system and it is easy to get overwhelmed. There are overt and obvious influences on human behavior like two separate buildings affecting communications between departments, and subtle, less obvious, influences such as one difficult employee or different ideas on what is good customer service. Not only could there be dozens of issues, but determining the root cause for all of them is a challenge and getting senior leadership to understand and buy into your recommendations is an even bigger challenge.

Identifying and sorting out the system influences is a diagnostic challenge, but an exciting one. Consider an organization like Walmart with 2,300,000 employees, and 10,586 stores in twenty-four countries, operating under forty-six different names, or the Department of Homeland security with 260,000 employees in twenty-two different agencies, each with their own cultures, rules, and regulations. Understanding how these systems influence human behavior is an exciting, multi-year endeavor.

Effective organization alignment is an alignment with the mission and purpose of the organization and with the values and vision. The more misaligned an organization, the more dysfunctional the organization. Large systems have many different parts that need alignment with the purpose of the organization. There are many organizations with significant misalignments, yet they are profitable, so they continue in the same pattern. Thus, despite the potential for increased engagement, morale, well-being, customer service, efficiency, etc., from increased alignment, pattern disruption can lead to less profitability and is then seen as undesirable.

CONCLUSION

In this chapter we define a system, indicate that organizations are systems and that there are models we can use to make sense of the system. We also discuss the differences between organization development and organization design when working within a whole system. Regardless of whether you emphasize organization design or development, good OD practitioners are systems thinkers, explore the root causes, and help clarify the ideal future state of organizations to scope their interventions.

QUESTIONS

1. Are you biased to practicing certain methods?
2. Why do you prefer a certain method?
3. Are you certain you can choose a method that best meets a client's need, rather than your personal preference?
4. Think about the organization you currently work with, what are the different elements of the system? How do those elements reinforce one another?
5. How do you view the differences between organization design and development? Do you use both in your practice?
6. When would focusing on design positively influence change in your organization?
7. Where would organization development best help influence the systems in your organization?

CHAPTER 3

Proactive and Reactive Organizations

Proactive: acting in anticipation of future problems, needs, or changes (www.merriam-webster.com, accessed July 19, 2023)

Reactive: of, or relating to, marked by a reaction or reactance (www.merriam-webster.com, accessed July 19, 2023)

Along with rapid changes such as the introduction of new technologies, the great resignation, the new hybrid workforce, and several other major shifts, there are ongoing day-to-day operations and problem-solving tasks. Many managers, leaders, and internal consultants find themselves striving to maintain operations and production while keeping the momentum going. Finding time to adopt a more strategic outlook, be proactive, or conduct a complete organizational review is becoming increasingly rare and consequently, there may be little significant sustainable organizational change.

Organizations often put band-aids on major problems, rarely addressing the root cause. **Organizations spend considerable time reacting to today's problems, rarely realizing that by reacting today, they may be creating tomorrow's problems.** While the concepts of proactivity and reactivity have been around for a very long time, they have not often been applied to organizations and Organization Development. This chapter will address the differences between proactive and reactive organizations, consulting, and management practices.

Proactivity involves anticipating and preparing for occurrences or situations before they happen, whereas reactivity involves responding to events as they happen, or after they happen. Proactive is more forward-looking while reactive is usually after the event has occurred. **Proactive OD is strategic or preventive, while reactive OD is responding to current circumstances or improving a situation that has already occurred.** The boundary between proactivity and reactivity is fluid and one can easily flow into the other. For example, is cultural change work proactive or reactive? Depends on whether it is in response to the current culture or trying to create a future culture. The defining factor may be the scope and focus of the individual consultant or the organizational initiative.

SCOPE/FOCUS

Organization Development practitioners are consulted for an exceptionally wide range of activities. Everything from the very broad cultural change, or system-wide organizational improvement initiatives, to the very focused singular activities, such as implementing one training program for a particular department. Determining the scope of the work and obtaining agreement on the same from senior management is important. This allows the practitioner to focus on the specific work and not be distracted by additional requests or project creep.

There is also a proactive and reactive focus. Reactive work tends to focus on improving some condition or fixing a current problem. Since organizations are frequently reacting to customer requests or environmental changes, it is natural that organizations are, in their attempt to remain agile, going to be constantly changing (reacting). A constantly changing environment leaves precious little time for strategic or long-range planning, so naturally the daily focus will most likely be both internal and limited in scope.

As written in our first book, "OD for the Accidental Practitioner," it bears repeating that **many organizations are caught up in responding to either symptoms or solutions and have not invested the time and energy to discover the root cause.** Responding to either the symptoms or the solutions tends to be reactive and does not lend itself to discovering the system's influences and root cause (proactive).

Three Statements

Juan, we have a problem in the shipping department where it seems there is a great deal of hostility and arguments. Can you please help the manager resolve these issues? SYMPTOM.

Juan, the shipping department apparently needs conflict resolution training as there are a lot of arguments and high levels of conflict. Can you please see what programs are available and affordable? SOLUTION.

Juan, apparently our shipping department has a fair amount of conflict and arguments. Would you please spend a few days talking to folks to see how serious this is, how long-standing it is, and what might be causing or influencing this situation? PROACTIVE.

Proactive OD focus will likely be external (e.g., on the customer or preventing future problems or reducing unintended consequences before they happen) or focus on the whole system. Substantive organizational change as well as sustainable organizational change requires a whole system focus.

Proactive OD focuses on all factors impacting the organization's entire system. Reactive work primarily addresses the organization's internal issues. To be clear, both need attention, neither one works to the exclusion of the other. However, determining the root cause is extremely challenging without a comprehensive view of the entire system. Proactive OD, Change Management, and HR have broad applications while reactive work tends to be more narrow or specific.

Proactive	**Reactive**
• Future change	• Current problem/issue
• Initiative, bigger picture	• Project, limited scope
• Root cause oriented	• Symptoms oriented
• Systems thinking	• Simple solutions/thinking
• Cause unknown	• Cause identified
• Preventative	• Band-aid

An OD consultant provides a higher value contribution through the proactive and preventative work they implement for an organization. Many internal and external OD consultants are called upon to accomplish reactive work. If an organization is bleeding, a band-aid (fixing the immediate problem) is a good first step. However, if that is all the consultants do, the entire organization will likely find themselves in a constantly reactive mode. Unfortunately, the underutilization of OD practitioners' proactive strategies often results from the organization's focus on crisis management or the execution of an executive's favored project.

One premise is that the organizational focus may well have something to do with the age of the organization. Many startups and family-run organizations (smaller organizations) are mainly focused on survival, gaining a foothold in the marketplace, sustaining, and ensuring their existence. Day-to-day activities, meeting payroll, dealing with customer complaints, ensuring quality and delivery tend to occupy their time, and looking five years down the road is a rare gift.

As an organization grows beyond 200 employees, its focus often shifts towards a more systematic and structured approach. Maybe an employee handbook gets developed, new reporting relationships emerge (organizational design), senior management is not as involved in the day-to-day operations, etc. The horizon is a little bit further out. As the company grows even further 2000+ employees, senior leadership is rarely involved in the day-to-day operations but addresses larger issues that will be due down the road such as market growth, mergers and acquisitions, divestitures, global reach and new products or ventures, green initiatives, public perception, etc. Larger organizations may have a greater need for OD professionals compared to smaller ones. However, there have been small and mid-size organizations that are proactive and looking further down the road, so it cannot just be a matter of organizational size or age, it may also be influenced by the leader's personality, type of business, mission of organization and a host of other factors as well.

Case in Point

The internal OD consultant was approached by the organization's president who was talking with a friend (another CEO) who stated that they were able to cut their turnover rate by as much as seventy percent in the last year due to a new and robust onboarding program. The CEO talked about numerous points of the onboarding program such as the importance of the first week, assigning big brothers and sisters to mentor the new employee, having all the necessary space and equipment that they will need to be successful on the job, exposing them to the organization mission, vision, and values, etc. The internal OD consultant was charged with researching other organizations with strong onboarding programs, taking the best from each and improving their own program with the goal of reducing their turnover rate which they considered high at about twenty-one percent. In fact, in some departments, turnover was as high as forty percent for first-year employees.

This is reactive OD at its finest. This request, while common, ignores the entire diagnostic process, does nothing to find the root cause of the turnover, and completely ignores other elements of the system that may be major contributors to the problem, such as culture, work practices, rules and regulations. While there is little doubt that onboarding programs can often be improved, and that may help with turnover, discovering and solving the root cause will truly solve the problem and not just put a band-aid on a major problem (twenty-one percent turnover). Also, the assumption that there is a single cause for the turnover (lack of a good onboarding program) is a risky supposition which often does not turn out to be true.

Before the organization spends a lot of time, money, and other resources trying to solve a nonexistent problem or implementing a solution that does not give the organization the results they are looking for, let's consider the following. What if at least part of the turnover problem was:

- The supervisors.
- Rules or regulations.
- The organization culture and its emphasis on speed over quality.
- Work fragmentation and no one saw the whole picture.
- Hostile competitive or negative work climate.
- Poor physical conditions/equipment.
- Long work hours, no work-life balance.
- Poor interviewing and employee selection.
- Compensation levels and bonus program.

There is no improved onboarding program in the world that will solve the above issues. The primary reason many OD initiatives fail to achieve all of their objectives, is the failure to identify the root cause or consider the entire system.

The real value the OD consultant can bring to this problem is to tell the executive that they will be happy to look at other onboarding programs and then challenge the CEO's proposed solution (onboarding) by saying, *"What if that is not OUR problem? What if our root cause lies elsewhere? You would not want me to waste resources doing something that will not give you the results you want,"* then help the executive define the results they are looking for, i.e., a fifty percent reduction in turnover. Once the end goal is established, the OD consultant can design an intervention that will help them uncover the root cause(s) and then design the appropriate intervention(s). This is proactive OD at its finest. It makes more sense to invest a little time and resources in identifying the root cause than to expend significant time and resources on addressing a nonexistent problem.

PROACTIVE AND REACTIVE CULTURES IN ORGANIZATIONS

The following exercise helps with understanding organizational culture and whether it is predominantly proactive or reactive. Once identified, examine the system's supporting factors, such as culture, policies, practices, rules, regulations, and management styles. More importantly, to change the culture, identify which system factors need addressing first and then look at what behaviors need to change as well.

WORD EXERCISE

Circle as many words/phrases that describe the culture of your organization or one you are working with.

Friendly	Slow paced	Busy	Chaotic
Thorough	Rigid	Collaborative	Trusting
Innovative	Conflicted	Happy	Positive
Contentious	Isolated	Entrepreneurial	Keep to self
Caring	Work-life balance	Fast paced	Inclusive
Fun	Growth minded	Curious	Rewarding
Career-oriented	Continuous learning	Welcoming	Relaxed
Rigid		Communicative	Challenging
Laid back	Transparent	Disjointed	Dysfunctional
Integrated	Business-like	Respectful	Demanding
Inclusive	Flexible	Everyone for self	Just a job
Honest	Cooperative	Passionate	Thoughtful
Toxic	Energetic	Stressful	Polite
Sensitive	Leaderless	Rule-oriented	Bureaucratic
Visionary	Boring	Hostile	Siloed
Mission driven	Customer-oriented	Work only focus	Profit-oriented
Fast-paced	Motivated	Quality driven	Unethical
	Safety minded		

Now for the ones you circled, please put a "P" by those that are proactive in nature and a "R" by those that are more reactive. Some may be both depending on the circumstances, in which case, pick the one that occurs most frequently. Based on this quick assessment, is your organization more proactive or reactive?

DOWNWARD SPIRAL

Reactivity begets reactivity and the cycle continues until people in the organization just accept the culture as fast-paced, never realizing that they are helping to create a culture that they may not like. It is a downward spiral. How many times have you tried to fix a problem and years later it is still there? Reactive decisions and actions do not usually address the root cause. In the short term, proactive OD work may take longer (systemic approach), but in the long run will save the organization's time and energy.

The downward spiral is often fueled by the rush to implement, solve, fix, or move on to more serious issues, the mindset of speed to market. **The illusion or sensation that a lot is getting done, a lot of issues are addressed, and a lot of problems are being solved is fueled by the belief that activity equals results, that change activity is equal to change and it is not**. But, once in the grip of quick fixes, and band-aid problem solving, it becomes difficult to change the mindset and behaviors associated with it. It becomes difficult to slow down, take time, look for the root cause and change whatever system's elements might be supporting the culture of speed and quick fixes. This flows against the paradigm of 'there is no time,' which is not true because we each have twenty-four hours a day.

PROACTIVE MANAGERS

When the consultant is engaged by a company, department or team, the managers within the unit can be either proactive partners with the consultant or reactive recipients of the consultant's efforts. Proactive managers work with the consultant to determine what roles they will play in the change initiative, how they might help the consultant be successful, and how they might help both during implementation and in follow-up. They do not give up control, are involved in making decisions, work with the consultant to ensure success and watch what the consultant does and how they do it so that they can do it later independent of the consultant.

Reactive managers might listen to what the consultant proposes and, even if in agreement, would shift the responsibility for implementation and producing results to the consultant and wait for the outcome. Even if the consultant is successful at producing results, there would be an increased dependency on the consultant for producing future results rather than the group learning about their processes and how to improve their own group dynamics. This is where the fifty-one percent concept really applies. The client must have at least fifty-one percent of the responsibility for the change initiative (OD for the Accidental Practitioner, 2022).

WHEN LEADERSHIP CHANGES

For the proactive OD consultant, internal or external, when there is a change in the executive positions, that is time to go to work. The likelihood that the new executive will keep the same initiatives, the same priorities, the same individuals on the team, and the same culture, is very rare to nonexistent. The proactive OD consultant will recognize the possibility of significant change and the impact on the organization, department, operations, and other staff before those impacts happen and help prepare both the executive his/herself and the team or organization in advance. At a minimum, they will be better prepared to react to the changes more quickly and decisively than if they just wait for the unintended consequences to occur.

Here are some common changes an organization can expect when leadership changes.

- *Change in personality.* Is the new executive more or less of a people person, more or less task-focused, more or less friendly, values-driven, communicative, trusting, competent, knowledgeable, team-oriented, etc.? How is this new executive different from the last one, and what are the anticipated effects on the remaining staff?

- *Change in both focus and priorities.* What is the probability that all the same initiatives will stay the same? Undoubtedly, some of the current initiatives will fall to the background and not have the same priority and some may end altogether. The new executive will likely have new ideas and want to implement new initiatives or have different priorities which will likely cause resistance among those responsible for implementing any changes. The "here we go again" syndrome can be especially demoralizing, especially in organizations like the military or government when change in leadership is mandated every two to four years. Worse still, what if the new executive's priorities would take the organization off track from its primary purpose or mission? Being able to speak truth to power may well be the most important trait of the proactive OD practitioner in such times.

- *Changes in relationships and power.* There is no question that there will be a dismantling of relationships and the establishment of new relationships, especially if the new executive is from the outside and brings in some of his/her own people. Which people will likely lose status, position, rank, authority and how will they, as well as the rest of the staff, be affected by the changes? Which individuals will receive a new authority, position or status and how will that affect everyone else? Who might quit or request a transfer and is that good or bad? How will this new executive interact with all the other executives and departments? What can the proactive OD consultant do to mitigate any negative impact of the new relationships?

- *Change in atmosphere and culture.* How will the working atmosphere or culture change? Will the atmosphere be more or less collaborative, trusting, open, friendly, communicative, etc.? Rest assured, the culture will change, will it be for the better or worse? How can the proactive OD consultant prepare the remaining staff for these changes? Is there sufficient infrastructure in place within the department to keep what is going well? What if the new executive is not a good fit for the department? What can the proactive OD consultant do to mitigate any negative impacts and reinforce the good aspects of the department?

Case Example – Impact of a new Director

For many years, in a city government department, there was a high degree of conflict, many union complaints, and significant employee dissatisfaction. When a new director was brought in to "fix" the department, he implemented many different practices and meetings and within two years completely turned this department around, making it one of the better-performing departments in the city government. He also wisely established numerous cross-functional teams to keep the process going after he left, knowing that he would be gone someday. In talking with the department some 20 years after the director departed and the organization had been through three other directors already, the department still used the initial cross-functional teams to address any problems the organization might have, and still maintained high morale and was even better performing than before. This demonstrates that if the right infrastructure is in place, it will outlast the executive in charge.

When a proactive OD consultant helps to establish a strong infrastructure, they work themselves out of the job of maintaining operations and can look forward to improving the future organization. Again, proactive OD at its finest.

Leadership is a strong influence on an organization's culture and operations, and any change in leadership will likely produce uncertainty and resistance. A proactive OD consultant will either anticipate the resistance, which is quite natural, or be ready for it when it occurs. How can the OD consultant support the incoming executive, yet support all the subordinates at the same time? What discussions or events need to take place prior to or immediately after a new executive is installed? Anticipating and responding to perceived or real problems in advance is proactive OD.

Case Example – Armee's Focus

Armee was an executive in Thailand and regional president. He was promoted to the president of worldwide operations based in Seattle WA. In the past five years, Armee successfully handled several lawsuits from environmental groups, two different plant catastrophes, one of a fire and another a building collapse, and several legal challenges by competitors. New government requirements on foreign workers, and a large amount of employee injuries and workman comp claims.

Due to his recent history, what is Armee likely to focus on?

Case Example – Alexis' Leadership

Alexis was born in a suburb of Perth Australia and spent much of her youth having to prove herself as a capable outdoor guide in the outback. She endured criticism from her male counterparts, especially those jealous of her capabilities. Alexis had an innate sense of direction and would never get lost, as well as a keen ability to perceive people's intent. She went to school at the University of Melbourne where she got her master's degree in finance and once again had to compete against a dominant male class. She graduated near the top of her class.

Growing up where she did and all of her experiences in her youth conditioned her to depend on herself and not to worry about the comments or evaluations of others. She became a rugged independent outback individual who was very capable of taking care of herself.

As a leader what will Alexis have a difficult time modeling?

COMPLEX AND INTERCONNECTED PROBLEMS

Because organizations are interconnected living ecosystems, there is rarely a single cause of a problem. Many organizational problems have numerous causes or influences. Without addressing all or most of the causes or influencers, there is a good likelihood that the problem(s) will recur. Reactive OD tends to fix (address) a problem with a potential solution, while proactive OD tends to change the influencers or the system that contributed to or caused the problem.

Case Example – Large Organization

A large organization (over 16,000 employees) requested services for one of its major units with three offices located in the Midwest, South and East Coast. The office in the Midwest was frequently in turmoil and there were many employee complaints. Employees were interviewed and the following information was discovered:

- *The director of this office was hated by many and supported by some.*
- *The main office realized that the director was a problem, but that director had been a loyal employee for almost 40 years and was due to retire soon. The main office was willing to let this person go out on their own terms.*

- *There were many subgroups among the employees given the small number of employees in this office. Even colleagues in the same jobs had subgrouping, and they were competitive and had conflictual relationships.*
- *The union was highly antagonistic.*
- *There were many employee complaints and several outstanding lawsuits.*
- *There were claims of racism and a hostile work environment.*
- *Many employees rarely came into work due to the hostile environment and instead chose to work from home with questionable productivity and no real means of measurement.*
- *There was little support and cooperation when the workload was heavy and subsequently, they could be several months behind on customer requests.*
- *One of the bosses at headquarters was also disliked because he would yell at people all the time.*
- *They were over the budget for many years due to excessive overtime when work was heavy.*
- *There was a limit on what customers could request so the customer submitted multiple requests under different categories to ensure they got the volume they needed but these multiple requests just increased the workload even further.*
- *There was low trust in everyone, especially in the external consultant who was hired by headquarters.*
- Where do you begin? Complex, yes. Interconnected, absolutely. Highly unlikely that any single or simple solution will fix this organization.

UNINTENDED CONSEQUENCES

Every single action has a consequence, just as every single nonaction has a consequence. In essence, there is always a consequence to everything you do or do not do. The simple definition of unintended is unplanned, or not previously thought of. So, what are unintended consequences? They are those actions or events that occur and were not anticipated or considered due to a previous action or nonaction. Since it is very difficult to think of every possibility before their occurrence, there are frequently unintended consequences, some severe and others not.

Case Example – Ship Maintenance

In U.S. history, there was a time when there was a push to reduce the military and in the Navy that meant fewer ships and less manpower. While some ships were decommissioned, others mothballed, and many active ships became more and more automated needing less and less personnel to work on the ships. The problem was that both ships that were mothballed and the ships that came in the shipyards for service, required more and more specialized maintenance personnel due to their automation and so the numbers of personnel increased rather than decreased even though there were fewer ships and fewer sailors on the ships.

If we find ourselves in a reactive mode, there is a greater likelihood of unintended consequences than if we

were to be in a proactive mode. The more we have time pressures to perform, the more we do not involve those affected by the change, the more we do not think of the whole system, the greater the likelihood of multiple and severe unintended consequences.

In a proactive mode, the change agent would consider all aspects of the initiative or change including the following:

- How will this change affect the entire organization?
- Who will it affect the most?
- Who needs to be involved?
- What might be all the consequences of this action (expected and unexpected)?
- Will this change require others to change as well?
- Is this a short-term or long-term solution?
- What is driving this change?

The need for speed may be slowing us down. In our rush to produce results, to hurry up change to stay competitive, we end up taking more time after the initial implementation and end up handling all the problems we did not consider before the implementation. When we do not consider the impact on others and invite them to the table to get their perspective, naturally we are going to miss many small details and their impact on those individuals. Frequently, senior management (in their mistaken wisdom) make decisions that they believe are good for the organization, only to find out that they were good for a limited group and not for the whole organization. Often these are financial or production decisions that may improve performance or save money but create many more issues than were solved.

An old oil filter ad for cars once advertised, "You can pay me now or pay me later," referring to the outcome, get your car oil changed now and pay for an oil change, or do not get your oil changed and you can pay later for an engine rebuild or a new engine. This is very apropos to organizational decision making and implementation. Take time to involve all necessary people now (proactive) or you will be spending time fixing the problems you created later (reactive). Once you accept that there always will be consequences to everything you do or do not do, then it becomes easier to identify all the potential consequences, greatly reducing the number of unintentional ones.

Case Example – Decentralized HR

A 5000-person organization with six regions spread across the US had HR people decentralized so that each region had their own HR staff they could rely on. Unfortunately, this resulted in very inconsistent advice between the regions and even within the regions because the advice you received depended on who answered the phone that day. Subsequently, each region had different rules and policies that at times were in direct conflict with one another.

Seeing the problem (actually, inconsistent information was not the problem, it was a symptom) management decided to relocate all the HR staff to one central location in New Mexico. Many millions of dollars were spent moving all employees and contracting for larger office space in New Mexico. They believed (correctly so) that this would facilitate HR personnel in building their own team, networking and improving the consistency of advice and policy formulation and implementation.

What was not anticipated was that over half of the staff did not want to move, so they quit and there was a need for massive hiring to bring in lots of new people. Additionally, the regions felt the moved HR personnel no longer knew their specific situation and that the advice they were now being given did not match their unique circumstance, so the region ended up hiring local HR assistants to replace the ones they lost, increasing organizational costs. The advice was still not totally consistent because all the new people and individuals did not know the policies. Additionally, many individuals who did move were not happy and became disgruntled employees.

The last thing you want is disgruntled HR employees who have to interact with all employees. Had senior management involved the regions, the organization may have decided that the move may not be THE solution to their problem but might be a solution or a part of a solution. Many individuals said afterwards that we could have told them this would happen had they asked for our input.

INVOLVEMENT

It is difficult, if not impossible, for any one person to realize or anticipate all consequences that might occur, therefore the need for others to be involved is critical. Those closest to the work know best, so their involvement is important to the change process. Often, a group of senior people, who are not involved in the hands-on day-to-day operations make operating decisions that affect the workforce, often with adverse unintended consequences.

Why is it that managers think they know better than those on the front line doing the work? Is it an "I know best" philosophy, "that is why I am the manager?" Is it the hierarchy that says those at the top make the decisions, and those at the bottom implement them? Is it the lack of consideration of others? Whatever the reason, it is a mistake to not involve those who will be affected by the decision. It is further a mistake to think that only a limited number of people will be affected by the decision. Organizations are intricately connected, and any change in one department affects all other departments, some, more severely than others. A proactive organization will always try to anticipate, address, and possibly eliminate problems before they occur.

Case Example – Hospitals and Insurance Requirements

A large hospital system had a group of contract physicians who work in utilization review, reviewing all hospital admissions. There were two categories, observation only and admission. The difference in what the hospital can bill insurance is very significant, so naturally hospitals want to have as many of the patients admitted as possible. On the other side of the issue are the insurance companies who want to pay the least amount possible and have a set of criteria that hospitals must meet for a patient to qualify for admission. There is a group of physicians that review each hospital stay and when the insurance company and the hospital disagree, a meeting is set up between the physicians who work for the insurance company and the hospital to discuss the case and see if it met the criteria for admissions. Peer-to-peer meetings took more time due to scheduling, phone tag, etc. Usually, it is worked out at that level, but if not, there is an appeal process and protocol, usually kicking the case up to the respective attorneys or senior medical staff of each institution.

In this one hospital system, there was a physician who was extremely detailed and careful in reviewing all medical records and when she thought that the patient did in fact meet insurance requirements would call the insurance company requesting a peer-to-peer meeting and had a 95% success rate in getting the insurance companies to agree to the admission of the patient. This one physician alone was responsible for saving the hospital several million dollars per year. However, there were many times she would agree with the insurance companies that the patient was only an observation rather than an admission patient because they did not meet the established criteria. The contracted physician received a set fee for reviewing the medical records and a higher set fee for peer-to-peer calls. It would have been to her financial advantage to take as many peer-to-peer calls as possible, but her ethics said to only do so when it was clear that the patient needed to be admitted.

Hospital administration began to realize that the more cases the physicians could turn into admission rather than observation, the more money the hospital could make. So, they began to require the physicians to do more peer-to-peer calls even on short-stay cases. This physician said to the hospital, "When I take questionable cases my success rate (ninety-five percent) will go down and I will be spending more time on one-to-three-day hospital stay cases rather than the five-to-fifteen-day cases which make the hospital more money." The hospital said to do it anyway. In other words, the hospital was incentivizing her financially to be less effective and make less money for the hospital. Overall, this physician was not able to save the hospital any more money. Even worse, this physician began to believe she was being asked to do things that she did not think was right and her enthusiasm for her role in the organization diminished to a job.

MOVING FROM A REACTIVE TO A PROACTIVE ORGANIZATION

Often, a culture of reactivity and a short-term focus is not a conscious decision, but a slow natural consequence of paying attention to the day-to-day issues that inevitably arise. It is a natural consequence of being responsive and responsible. Over time, however, when the focus can, should, or might shift, it does not. By then, it has become a habit to deal with the immediate. The immediate still needs attention, it cannot be ignored, but who pays attention to the immediate and who pays attention to the more strategic (long-term focus) is what is at question here.

Phil's Case

Phil was the proud owner of a small lawn and garden company (forty-five employees) and was a forward-thinking individual. He wanted to provide his six supervisors with customer service training. A time was arranged to discuss his goals and what might be included in the curriculum. On the day and time of the meeting, the consultant was present, but Phil was not. He had come into the office early that day to prepare for the meeting, but one of his trucks broke down and he went out to fix it. Now, at what point does the president/owner of a company say that fixing trucks is not the best use of his time? His rationale was that he knew the equipment better than anyone else and therefore was the best person to fix them. While this may be true, the consequences of these actions are:

- *He will limit the growth of his company based on the number of hours he can work.*

- *He will likely become the bottleneck in the company by trying to do everything.*

- *He will adopt a micro-management style.*

- *He will inadvertently train his people to not take responsibility for making decisions and reverse delegate them to him.*

- *The immediate need will take priority over the important, and the company will likely develop a habit of short-term focus.*

Typically, as a company grows, the founder who loved doing the work, now finds themselves running the office, paying bills, answering inquiries, and dealing with paper. They will often state that the job is not fun anymore, that they would rather be out doing the work, having contact with their customers, etc. This is a natural progression. The next step is for the owner to get other managers/supervisors (office manager) to handle the necessary paperwork; but, and this is critical, not go back into doing the work, but become more long-term (strategic) in their focus. This is not just a small company issue; large companies are just as subject to this short-term focus as the following two cases suggest.

The consequence of a short-term focus is that the organization or individuals are enabling tomorrow's crisis and perpetuating the short-term focus. They are in a never-ending downward spiral. How then, does the OD practitioner help an organization/client shift from short-term to long-term, or at least some combination of the two?

Training and development can help. Training all managers/supervisors in the types of decision-making is a reasonable start. There is simple thinking and decision-making, it is a simple cause-and-effect type of thinking, short-term focus often referred to as band-aid thinking. So, if I pick up a garden implement and cut my hand on a metal burr, I go get a band-aid to stop the bleeding. In simple thinking and decision-making, I have solved the problem, and appropriately so. Some people think that they are doing more strategic thinking if they prepare for the same simple solution in advance. In this example, it would be the person who realizes they need to use that implement a lot over the next several weeks, so they better obtain a large supply of band-aids.

In systemic thinking, look for the root cause (i.e., the metal burr). Take a grinder and grind down the metal burr, or use a different implement and in both cases, eliminate the need for additional band-aids. This addresses the root cause.

Strategic or preventative thinking and problem solving would look ahead and prevent the problems before they occur. In this case, an individual might realize they need to use several different implements and in order to avoid any potential hand injuries, wear a good pair of gloves whenever using tools (OD for the Accidental Practitioner, 2022).

In Phil's case (above), he might need to solve the immediate problem (fix the broken truck) and that might be the quickest solution today. It is a good example of simple thinking, but for a more systemic solution, he may have to develop clear policies on truck breakdowns, and who is responsible for fixing the trucks. Provide training for the supervisors so that not all day-to-day problems end up on the president's desk. He would benefit from establishing a culture where individuals are encouraged to make decisions, do not get punished for making mistakes and take more responsibility as important team members in the organization.

QUESTION EVERY SOLUTION

Make it standard practice, the norm, to question every solution.

1. Is this really a solution to our problem?
2. What other solutions can we come up with? Never settle for just one solution. The rules of brainstorming work well here.
3. Will this solution give us all or just some of the results we are looking for?
4. What unintended consequences might occur?
5. Are we just treating the symptom and not the root cause?

GAUNTLET OF SUSPICION

Have every major decision run the gauntlet of suspicion. Question if this is a poor, good, great decision or even a decision at all. Ensure that the solution will solve all aspects of the problem. Also, ensure that it will not create additional problems elsewhere in the organization. Eliminate blame and who owns the idea. In challenging organizations, **it is not who is right, but what is right for the organization.**

In scientific studies, there is the theory of falsifiability (Popper, 1956) which essentially states that if your theory can be refuted or disproved, then it is a false theory. It is significantly easier to accept that your solution is a poor solution when you come to that conclusion before others do. Challenge your own thinking and problem-solving. Strong interference, another approach to scientific assessment, advocates the need for multiple hypotheses rather than a single hypothesis to avoid simplistic thinking and confirmation bias (Platt, 1962).

Taking the extra time to prove your solution will get you the results you are looking for is a good first step. Having additional potential solutions reduces the possibility of mistakes, unintended consequences, and resistance to change. Furthermore, having multiple solutions is more proactive while having only one solution is more reactive problem-solving.

LONG-TERM PERSPECTIVE

The statement, "Yesterday's solutions are today's problems" is very true. When being reactive and in simple thinking, we implement a new rule or process to solve an immediate problem, without regard for the longer-term impact or how it might affect others in the organization.

Case Example – Customer Service

The customer service department of a large corporation received many complaints that their agents took too long to answer calls and the customers were on terminal hold for long periods. Some wait as much as forty-five minutes. Customer service was rated very low by eighty-three percent of all customer surveys. Only three percent rated customer service as high or very good. To improve customer service, a new rule was designed by corporate that no customer was to wait on hold for more than ten minutes, and they would get a phone system that announced wait times to their customers giving them the option to receive a callback. Problem solved; you say?

To ensure that all calls were handled under the ten-minute wait period, all agents became more abrupt, and quick to get those on the phone call off so they could get to the next one. The ten-minute mark was reached within two months of policy implementation, but customer service declined even further, but for different reasons. Simple thinking, short-term focus, reactive problem-solving at its finest.

Always question, "If we implement this solution…"
1. What possible long-term consequences will we incur?
2. What other problems might we create?
3. How will this affect other departments within the organization?
4. What rules, regulations, values, or processes might this be violating?

5. What consequences will we incur if we do not implement this solution?

'WHAT ARE WE NOT SEEING' SESSIONS

Some organizations have brainstorming sessions, others have implementation teams, and some have challenge sessions where an idea is looked at and challenged by everyone to see if it can stand the test of the gauntlet. While these sessions take time in the front end, they generally save time during implementation because there is less resistance to the initiative by employees that have been part of the planning process as well as fewer unintended consequences.

PAY ATTENTION – NOW

Proactive OD will look at as many aspects of the problem as possible, while reactive OD tends to have a narrow focus, i.e., fixing the problem. One area of questioning would be to determine why we are addressing this problem now. Did someone just discover the problem recently, or has this problem been an ongoing concern for some time? If so, then why are they paying attention to it now? What is the driving force behind fixing this issue and how does that affect either the problem or the solution, or both?

If the problem has existed for some time, then in some way the system has supported, tolerated, or endured this behavior for some time. What policy, procedure, practice, process, or individuals might need to change to support the new desired behaviors? It might be as simple as changing a policy or practice or holding people accountable or it might be as complex as having to work first on system change and then on behavioral change as well as any resistance to change.

CONCLUSION

In this chapter, we introduced the concepts of proactive vs. reactive organization development and discussed how these two concepts emerge in organizations and influence the work of OD practitioners. While many organizations seek OD practitioners to support a reaction to a problem (reactive), it is beneficial to turn the reaction into an ability to be proactive. Proactive OD entails a long-term perspective and helps practitioners and leaders alike to remember why they are seeking change and how to sustain it.

CHAPTER 4

From Reactive to Proactive

In OD, we will likely be called when a client becomes aware of and reacts to a problem. It is a rare leader who wants to do a health check on an organization that is running optimally. This means practitioners are regularly faced with helping to turn a reaction into a proactive approach within an organization. Here, we propose some instances where this emerges and options for the intentional practitioner.

URGENCY

Pressure, stress, critical deadlines, and the need for speed in hitting quarterly goals are all factors that create a sense of urgency, compelling leaders to act swiftly. These leaders are under the close scrutiny of senior management or the Board of Directors, with their bonuses and longevity at the company riding on their performance—financially, interpersonally, and in terms of growth and efficiency.

This urgency is not just about dealing with the task at hand but extends to problem-solving. The approach is straightforward: identify the problem, solve it quickly, and move on to the next, in a culture that values quick fixes and immediate results. This mindset encourages simple, reactive solutions, reflecting the organization's overall emphasis on speed and urgency.

Whether you are an internal or external consultant, you may find that you are frequently requested to fix an issue, respond to a current situation, or improve a current condition. In other words, the problem already exists, it is no longer preventable, and other pressures may now exist for an immediate response. The first step in providing proactive consulting is to get clarity on the problem, and what is being asked of you. The following questions help obtain that clarity.

- If you are being asked to fix a problem, or improve a situation, is there a clearly defined problem?
- What is the history of this problem?
- What or who might possibly be supporting or enabling the problem?
- How long has the problem existed?
- Has any solution been suggested or previously implemented?
- What are the consequences of not fixing the problem?
- What is this problem costing the organization?
- Can we come up with more than one solution?
- How will any solution affect any other department?
- Who else needs to be involved?
- Are sufficient resources being allocated to fixing this problem?
- Do you have sufficient authority and support to fix the problem?
- How will senior leadership be involved?

The second step is to attempt to restructure or broaden the assignment so that it includes root cause analysis or system improvement as well as relationships or skill improvement. There are many creative ways to be compliant with the request and subtly shift the focus from reactive to proactive consulting work, here are some examples.

- Agree to the assignment starting with a diagnostic to ensure you have a solid grasp of the current situation. Commit to a report back to management within "X" weeks reporting what you found and your recommendations on how to proceed. Essentially, this is starting with a diagnostic data collection process and the involvement and action planning with senior leaders.

- Begin by forming a problem-solving group involving all stakeholders who might be affected by any changes.

- Break the project up into phases, giving management reports along the way including your next steps, time frame, and necessary resources.

- Get clarity around the time frame and, if unrealistic, put the issue on the table. Such phrases as "I think we can get the results you are looking for, but not in the time frame you're requesting, what do you think we should do?" are powerful attention-getters and help reorient the project scope.

- Confront the issue directly that you think the request is a simple stop-gap type of thinking and decision-making and you believe it to be necessary to get to the root cause first. Discuss or demonstrate the types of decision-making and if possible, give examples the corporation has experienced previously.

- Engage senior leadership in discovering potential unintended consequences and discuss actions to mitigate the same.

- Involve those who will be affected by the change and get their opinions before we get too far into an expensive change process.

- Ask them to spend a little time and money assessing the situation before spending a lot of time and money fixing something that does not need to be fixed or fixing the wrong thing.
- A further step is politely or diplomatically declining the assignment as is, especially if you believe the assignment has no chance of success under the current circumstances. These are the projects that are doomed to fail from the start. There, unfortunately, are a considerable number of these projects. Many more than most of us would like to see. They are often underfunded, under-resourced or unrealistic in what can be accomplished with the solution that is offered.
- When the consultant encounters a project that s/he knows will not give the organization the results they are looking for, it poses a dilemma. Do you:
  o Accept the project in the hopes that you can do some good or make a difference?
  o Accept a part of the project leaving open the possibility of discussion on the remaining parts?
  o Refuse the project and risk the consequences?
  o Inform the group why you think the project will not succeed and attempt to alter it so that it will succeed?
  o Not inform the group why you think the project will fail but work to alter it so that it will succeed?
  o Other.

An OD consultant's decisions are influenced by their sense of security, economic considerations, personal values, and circumstances. However, adopting a pessimistic outlook towards a project's success can be self-fulfilling, leading to subpar performance or failure. This raises important questions: Why commit your time, energy, and reputation to a cause that's doomed from the start? Shouldn't the consultant's primary focus be the best interest of the organization or client? At the heart of OD practice is the principle that all efforts should aim to enhance both the organization's effectiveness and the well-being of its people?

As demonstrated in the following case, external consultants may have a difficult time refusing an assignment for economic reasons but have an easier time refusing an assignment for political or practical reasons. Internal consultants will likely be engaged in many projects and therefore refusing one assignment will not have much, if any, financial impact on them, (they will still have a job) but may have a more difficult time refusing an assignment for political or relationship reasons.

Case Example – Is Training Really the Solution?

An organization has requested that you conduct a series of brief training programs on a variety of predetermined topics. Upon inquiry about the purpose and selection of these topics, it was revealed that they were chosen by senior management without clear explanations for their choices. The organization's goals for these trainings were unclear, offering only vague aspirations like "to improve our employees." Furthermore, the employees are currently unaware of the upcoming sessions.

Regarding the implementation and follow-up of the training, the expectation seems to be that employees will independently use the information provided to become better-informed.

You assess this situation as potentially ineffective and inefficient due to the absence of clear objectives or identified needs the training is supposed to address. Despite being familiar with the topics, preparing for these sessions will require significant effort, including creating printed materials and PowerPoint slides, coordinating with the organization's internal training department, and managing logistics. This preparation is anticipated to demand approximately six full days of your time per session, including delivery, alongside additional administrative and minor travel arrangements.

Despite the offered compensation of $20,000.00 per program, significantly higher than your usual fees, you are concerned about the value and impact of the training given the lack of direction and measurable outcomes. What do you do?

WHEN A SOLUTION IS NO SOLUTION

When requested to implement a solution that you do not think will give the organization the desired results **take away the solution**. A solution that does not solve the problem is not a solution at all, so take it off the table and continue discovery efforts on what the problem is, what the organization wants, what behaviors will need to change, what in the system currently supports the dysfunctional behavior, etc.

A dialogue might go like this:

Reggie: *Susan, we have two departments that are constantly at each other's throats, arguing constantly, and always blaming each other. If we get their leadership* *together, can you give them a brief training program on conflict resolution?*

Susan: *Certainly, this can be done, but may I ask a few questions first? When you say "brief" what are you thinking time-wise?*

Reggie: *Maybe one to two hours, three at the most. I do not want to take them off work too long, given their tendency to argue a lot.*

Susan: *(Now at this point Susan knows that this will do little good, and may even cause more problems than it fixes) Reggie, when you say, "their leadership," how many people are you thinking would participate and would this be the leadership from all shifts?*

Reggie: *Yes, all shifts and anyone from supervisor on up.*

Susan: *Roughly how many people would that be?*

Reggie: *Well, there are roughly four to five supervisors in each department, one operational manager, one department manager, and one quality manager in each department on days and slightly less on swing shift, so my best guess is about twenty-five to thirty people. But you can go to HR and look at who you think should be invited and make a list and let me see it.*

Susan: *Do any of the managers get along with one another or do they all argue with each other?*

Reggie: *I am not sure.*

Susan: *Do the departmental employees argue as well or not? Should they be a part of this program?*

Reggie: *Actually, the employees seem to cooperate far better than the managers. I think it is mostly the managers.*

Susan: Why do you think that the employees seem to work well with one another, but the managers do not?

Reggie: I am not sure, maybe it is because the employees must work together to get the job done, but the supervisors do not.

Susan: Who do these two departments report to at headquarters?

Reggie: Well, one reports to marketing and the other reports to operations, and these two senior executives don't get along all that well either.

Susan: So maybe the supervisors and managers are merely modeling the senior leaders' behaviors, in which case, training in conflict resolution may not be the answer but working with various individuals to resolve their differences and be more supportive of one another is. Would you be open to getting the same results you want if it could be done through another means?

Reggie: If these groups stop arguing and blaming one another however you accomplish that, it is fine with me.

Susan: Let me spend a little time collecting more information, then I will develop a plan and we can sit down then and finalize what will be best for everyone. Are you OK with this?

Reggie: Sure, how long do you need to develop a plan?

Susan: I will have it within three weeks and if I can make it sooner, I will let you know.

Reggie: The sooner the better and thanks for your time today.

Susan skillfully took the solution, Conflict Resolution Training, off the table by a series of questions, essentially using the discovery interview process (OD for the

Accidental Practitioner, 2022). Susan knew that this was not a lack of skills issues that would respond well to a training initiative, but something else in the system was supporting the arguing and blaming behaviors. Most likely senior management, but through a brief diagnostic, Susan will likely be able to figure out the root cause and then design an initiative to truly solve the problem. It is a difficult problem for Susan because it is unlikely that the employee behaviors will change unless senior management does and if they do not, will the senior executives be willing to step in and make the necessary changes?

Once a solution is thought of, there is a tendency by many individuals to stop all further thinking. One and done. Then there is a rush to implementation. If you take the given solution off the table, you are left with the problem to explore further to make sure that there is a problem, that the fix is not worse than putting up with the problem, that the fix is the right fix, that there may be other fixes equally as good or better. etc. Take the time to do it right and avoid the adage **"why is there never enough time to do it right but always enough time to do it over?"**

CREATIVE REFUSAL

Case Example - Raja

Raja worked as an internal OD consultant for a large corporation, (7600 employees). His boss Nahar came to him with a solution for the accounting department which was to provide Excel training to all new and current employees. The accounting department had four divisions, taxes, employee compensation, executive compensation, accounts receivable and accounts payable. Raja was not sure why the boss wanted the training and only got a general answer "because they need it." When he questioned even further, he was essentially told to just get a vendor and provide the training within the next 60 days. Not wanting to upset his boss, he said he would look into it.

Raja then discussed the training with the four managers, and they all said that it would be a waste of company resources. Many of their people already knew Excel very well, in fact, could teach it, some did not use it in their jobs, and others were far too busy to take time out for training. Raja was sure at this point that any training would not be received well, would be an unproductive use of employee time, costly, and unnecessary. His boss, however, was demanding that he contract for the training.

Raja's next step was to invite several employees from each group to help him develop a curriculum and essentially got the same response as he did from the managers: unnecessary, poor use of time, already using the program, not having the need for the program, too busy. Raja reported this to Nahar and once again, but more angrily, got the same response, "Get it done."

Raja was absolutely certain that this was a complete waste of time and money, would solve nothing, probably cause more harm than good, further anger employees, and produce no real benefit to either the organization or their customers. He was ready to go in and confront his boss.

Raja's Solution
It was then that Raja hit upon a creative solution. He found an online tutorial of Excel basics that took less than

one hour to view and at the end had five brief questions. If you could demonstrate that you already can answer these five questions, you did not have to listen to the tutorial. You could also just look up the answers to these five questions, but all employees had to take the test. He sent out an email with instructions to all employees in the accounting department. He reported back to Nahar that the training was made available to employees and that 99% of all employees took the test with a 97% passing rate. Nahar was satisfied and there was no further discussion regarding the training.

The balance between being a dutiful employee and living according to your values can be difficult. Do you do what you're told to do believing that this is being a good follower even though you are confident that it will not work, or do you do what you know and believe is the right thing to do? It appears that Raja found a middle ground.

Case Example - Carla

Carla was asked to work with two recently merged large departments to integrate their work. This involved a reassignment of roles and responsibilities, a reduction in supervisors, an integration of different technologies, a physical move to another building by some team members, a status and title change by a few of the senior leaders, and the development of newly formed subgroups. This is what was known, but what was yet to surface was Carla's big concern. The time frame for complete integration was 120 days. It was Carla's estimate that this integration could easily take a year or longer. Carla did not want to start a project she could not complete or do well. Her reputation was at stake. She pushed back hard on management's time frame, yet they were insistent, believing that it could be done in 120 days and that if Carla needed help, she should get it from HR.

Carla then said she would do the first phase which was to collect data from the two groups on what they thought the priorities were and how they might help her. Based on that data, she would report what she had found out and together they would craft a plan of action going forward keeping in mind the 120-day time frame. As anticipated, the attitude of employees was skeptical, fearful, non-trusting, scared, angry, and bewildered. People were afraid of losing their jobs, many had updated their resumes and sent them out to recruiters and social media apps. Employee attitudes were so negative that it surprised the senior leadership who thought highly of the merger (naturally, it was their idea). Based on this negativity and fearfulness, they removed their 120-day time frame and Carla was given complete authority to do what it takes to have a successful merger.

When Carla realized that what they were asking her to do was accompanied by an impossible and unrealistic time frame, she planned to involve senior management as quickly as possible so that they could see firsthand and be involved and informed. She knew that if it was as bad as she thought, and there were many major tasks to accomplish that senior leadership would soon see the folly of their time frame and that is exactly what happened.

CONCLUSION

This chapter discussed how practitioners can help a client move from reactive to proactive interventions. In fact, sometimes it is possible to refuse to act on the ideas presented by a client and instead suggest alternative actions that a client is willing to accept. Consider what you have read here and think about how you can help a client move from a reactive situation to a proactive one. What would you recommend and what skills would you apply?

CHAPTER 5

Interventions

Deciding when, how, and whom to involve in client interventions requires careful consideration due to the complexity of organizational systems and the diverse consequences that interventions can trigger. Given the prevalence of this understanding, it begs the question: Why do so many professionals overlook these dynamics in their Change Management, Training and Development, Organization Development, Strategic Planning, or Decision-Making processes?

Interestingly, McKinsey & Company's 2015 analysis reveals that 70% of change initiatives fall short of achieving their full objectives. This statistic is often misconstrued, leading many to believe that 70% of all change initiatives outright fail—an interpretation that misses the nuance of partial success versus total failure. This discrepancy highlights a significant issue in the field: a systematic overlook of integral systems or a failure in change management efforts to fully meet their goals.

This chapter delves into the various reasons behind this oversight and the frequent underachievement of change initiatives. It aims to shed light on the critical yet often neglected aspects of organizational change, offering insights into how a more holistic and system-aware approach could improve the success rate of these endeavors.

CONSULTANT/PRACTITIONER

Relying on the consultant for answers generally increases the organization's dependency on the consultant, but a good facilitator, a process-oriented practitioner, will ask questions and facilitate discussion so the organization arrives at the answers it needs by themselves or with very little help from the practitioner.

The skills and competencies needed to perform a task lie within the individuals. If, however, the organization changes its structure, strategy, vision, manufacturing, or other key elements of the system requiring new skills and competencies, the organization will not change unless the people develop those new skills and competencies. **If people don't change, the results won't either.** However, if you develop those new skills and competencies before any organization change, and the system does not support the new abilities of the individual or there is no opportunity to use the new abilities, then they will likely be forgotten by the time the organization changes and the new abilities are needed. Change the system first, then work on human capabilities and performance.

When the need for new skills and competencies arises, it's essential to begin with leadership. Leaders must model these new requirements for their staff. If leaders fail to develop these competencies, the organization faces tough choices. Once leadership embodies these skills and supports the new direction verbally, it's easier for staff to follow suit. Ideally, leadership should be trained first, setting a precedent for the rest of the organization.

It is also critical that all leaders support the new culture, vision, strategy, or change initiative, otherwise you have unequal departmental support which tends to generate competition and conflict rather than collaboration. Getting all leaders to be on board can take a year or longer in organizations that have had a history of conflict or individualism. When there is internal conflict, it is difficult, if not impossible, to be a high-performing organization. It is analogous to a football team coming out of the huddle and every player has a different idea of what the next play is. They will be quite fragmented and dysfunctional in their execution.

Focusing solely on individual behavior without considering the system's influence often leads us to simplistic cause-and-effect solutions. By only tweaking the individual or a single system element, achieving the desired outcomes becomes unlikely. This approach is analogous to adjusting just one spoke on a bicycle wheel and expecting the wheel to be perfectly round afterward.

WORK INTEGRATION

According to Wilfrid R. Bion, (Psychoanalyst, president of the British Psychoanalytical Society_1962 to 1965), an individual's behavior can only be understood within the context of the groups in which they live. This underscores the principle that systems shape human behavior. Therefore, altering the system will affect both the individuals within it and the system itself.

Similarly, any change to one part of the system will likely influence other parts of the system. After all, the organization is an integrated whole. Proactive Organizational consultants recognize that whatever they do must be integrated into the whole system if it is going to be sustainable. Further, they anticipate, to the extent possible, the consequences of their change initiative on other parts of the system or the individuals within the system.

SOLUTIONS

Many people believe that if there is a problem, then there must be a solution. Just like cause and effect, there is a problem <u>and</u> a solution. In fact, the very idea that there might not be a good solution is foreign to some individuals. A manager may even believe that at least part of their job is to find solutions for any problems that arise. Problem solving in some organizations is a highly valued skill that goes on one's list of yearly accomplishments or is written into their performance reviews. Employes are given praise and written up in the employee newsletter for finding the solution to an organization problem that has plagued the organization for years. Their solution is extolled for having saved the company money or reducing expenses or improving customer service, quality, efficiency, or some other organizational aspect.

What if there are no solutions to some of the organizational issues we encounter, only adaptations? That the oxymoron "constant change" is the norm, and that speed of change and flexibility are highly valued. So instead of solutions, we have adaptations. The word "solutions" has a finality to it, while "adaptations" does not. Adaptation has a temporary time frame associated with it as well as a flexibility mindset.

Case Example – Scientist Communications

A scientific agency with highly educated individuals wanted their scientists to communicate better with one another. While the consultant encountered a lot of pushback by the employees saying that they were all too busy for any training program (training was decided as the solution) the organization did settle on a "lunch and learn "program that was only 90 minutes in length, once every other week for eight months. Not only would each session have a topical focus, but it would be a good opportunity to get to network and get to know others in the session which had 80 scientists in a large fixed chair auditorium. The program cost $250,000, not counting lost time, and ended up being a waste of time and money and helped establish a negative attitude toward training and management.

The organization's change initiative not only fell short of achieving its intended goal, but also resulted in adverse outcomes. Essentially, the organization invested a quarter of a million dollars only to deteriorate its situation. Not at all uncommon. In their drive to come up with a solution to their problem, they came up with the wrong solution, did not clearly define the problem and its consequences, determine the root cause, or identify major system influences such as the heavy pressure on scientists to publish first before sharing any data with anyone nor identify any other number of solutions that might have given them the results they are looking for. This is another common mistake regarding a solutions mindset and that is that there is only one solution.

Opting for a single solution carries a greater risk of selecting an incorrect approach compared to considering multiple solutions. Once a particular solution is identified, it often halts further creative thought. This is akin to a classroom scenario where a teacher confirms an answer to a question, effectively ending any additional thinking on the part of the students. Similarly, in business meetings, declaring a definitive solution can prematurely close off further discussion and exploration. Perhaps, instead of seeking a "once and for all" final answer, we should aim for a series of adaptations that gradually lessen the negative effects of the issue at hand.

Neuroscience tells us that the brain, while only being about three percent of our total body weight consumes about twenty percent of our daily energy (glucose and oxygen), so naturally the brain works to conserve energy. Thinking requires a lot of energy, so having a quick solution means that I do not have to think anymore since we already have an answer. How convenient.

There is a totally different aspect to the solutions narrative and that is the consultant's experience. If the consultant is an expert in project management with their PMP certification, then they tend to see the need for project management training everywhere they look. If my only tool is a hammer…

We once had a consultant who was delivering a training program in a series of supervisory training programs for a client. His recommendation for the next training program for this client was to do interpersonal skills training. After pushing the consultant for the "why" or reason for his recommendation, it finally came down to "I teach it so well."

While probably true, it is not a good reason why we should recommend anything to a client. This is a perfect example of recommending what we do best, not what is best for the client.

BINARY THINKING

Another matter of convenience is having only one or two positions. Things are either up or down, in or out, black or white, right or wrong, left or right, good or bad, for or against whatever. It certainly makes the world simple. You are either with me or against me. Unfortunately, the solutions to today's complex problems do not lend themselves very well to binary thinking, but to a deeper analysis of all the factors/positions affecting a decision. Once again, binary thinking tends to conserve a lot of energy, which makes it attractive to the brain. Binary thinking seeks an answer or position, while creative thinking seeks possibilities and alternatives, but requires more mental exertion. **Binary thinking tends to give us answers and creative thinking tends to give us questions.**

Binary thinking also tends to encourage competition where one position is superior to the other. I am right and you are wrong, I am taller and you are shorter, I have the right answer and you are wrong. Further, when we adopt a singular position, we are more likely to employ confirmation bias and only look for those things that support our position rather than be open to other possibilities. We become dismissive of anyone or anything that does not hold our position, or we do not see or look for other possibilities.

Binary thinking frequently steers us towards simplistic, expedient, short-term solutions rather than fostering comprehensive, systematic review, and root cause analysis. This approach oversimplifies complexities by restricting our choices to mere 'for' or 'against', devoid of any middle ground or room for nuance. As a result, the world appears less intricate, and our decision-making becomes constrained by binary options, stifling opportunities for exploring alternative perspectives and finding more holistic solutions.

BINARY THINKING AND EMOTIONS

Could it be that the more emotional the issues, the more we enter into binary thinking? Take any highly emotional issue like abortion, gun control, climate change, and politics, it seems as if people are firmly locked in one camp or the other, there is very little middle ground thinking, if any. High levels of emotions generally signal more meaningfulness, more intensity, and more attachment to the position or item.

When individuals are highly emotional, logic or scientific persuasion alone is unlikely to change their positions. Addressing their emotions first is crucial. Once they have calmed down, logic can be introduced with greater success. When people are intensely emotional, they are often closed off to alternatives and may even refuse to think about alternative solutions or courses of action. It is their way or no way (i.e., binary). Emotionally charged individuals (or groups) are often reactionary. During challenging times, a proactive consultant can provide immense value by prioritizing emotional awareness. By acknowledging and addressing emotional concerns first, the consultant can create a foundation of trust and understanding. Subsequently, they can gradually introduce proactive choices or courses of action, leveraging this emotional connection to facilitate constructive progress.

TIME

Speed to market, especially in the technology sector is important. Being the first to come out with a new and innovative product or service generally captures market share and the income generated from those first few years can soften the enormous research and development costs that go into creating a new product or service. Also, ever since the late 1990s when doing more with less became popular, most executives today are responsible for more projects than can realistically be accomplished by two or more executives.

So, we do not have a lot of time to spend on root cause analysis, or talking to entry-level employees, especially when we are convinced that we already know what the problem is. Companies today are often looking for the pill, the quick fix, the next big thing in management, etc. Taking quick and decisive action is admired, encouraged, and incentivized. Many organizations have a solution before they even know what the problem is.

Case Example – Team Building

Years ago, we received a phone call from an HR department asking us if we did "teambuilding." The short answer was yes, we had several staff that had these skills and methods as one of their strengths. However, we know that the term "teambuilding" means lots of different things to different people, so upon further inquiry, we tried to determine exactly what they were looking for. Was it conflict resolution, getting to know one another, establishing mutual goals, values, purpose, improving their group processes (aka Truckman model), high and low rope experiences, etc.? This individual was not quite sure which approach would be best, so we moved on from describing the various types of teambuilding we typically use, to having her describe the situation they were trying to improve. After ten minutes of attempting to describe what she thought was the reason for the team building, she finally said, "Well, I am not sure why we need team building, my boss just asked me to see who offered it."

So once again, a solution is recommended without any knowledge of the problem, root cause, or what the organization is trying to improve.

Organizational change, when executed effectively, is a costly and time-consuming endeavor, often exceeding initial expectations. This is largely attributed to the multitude of unforeseen challenges that arise during the implementation phase, revealing unknown factors that were not apparent at the outset of the change initiative.

As such, the two-month diagnosis becomes four months, and the two-week action planning session becomes three months due to the resistance to change and the inability to get a majority agreement. Frustrations arise due to the slow pace (even though they may be the cause of the slow pace) and the allocation of resources and expenses rise, causing some executives to rethink their support. This is where managing expectations and client relationships is critical to effectively engaging in change and the development process.

Cost

Finding the root cause and/or organizational analysis takes time, money, and people resources away from other, often critical, business tasks. It is not unusual for there to be a four-to-eight-month analysis period before senior leaders receive any information. Organizations occasionally believe they do not have the time to devote to such an effort and see the analysis as an unnecessary cost since they already believe they have a good idea of what the problems are. Foolishly, many organizations rush to spend money on a solution that, at best, is only a partial solution rather than spend a little bit of money up front making sure they have a problem at all or ensure they are solving the right problem. Solutions that do not work are not solutions and instead are often costly endeavors.

An organizational analysis can be costly. Some analyses include looking at the organization design, technology, quality, efficiency, customer service, leadership and management, internal DEI initiatives, green initiatives, as well as employee interviews. These reports usually fill a three-to-four-inch binder full of lots of charts and graphs and various ways to look at the same information. If you are a data junkie, these reports are fantastic sources of information, but if you are charged with improving the organization, the report does little to effect change past the first step of data collection. The senior leaders still need to prioritize the issues and decide which ones they will support in the coming months, decide on how to proceed with each of them, who will lead the effort, and then comes months of implementation.

INEXPENSIVE SOLUTIONS

Organizations often resort to several actions to create the illusion of addressing an issue, including:

- Forming a committee to conduct further investigation into the matter.
- Delegating the issue to specific groups such as HR, Quality, Security, etc.
- Implementing a training program aimed at addressing the issue.
- Facilitating discussion groups to explore and discuss the issue in depth.

These activities often have discovery value, but rarely lead to long-term organizational changes. However, they are not costly compared to a longer-term change process and can give the organization quick results they can report to management. They often give the illusion that something is being done about the problem, but the problem usually remains. These solutions tend to be activity-oriented, not result-oriented, reactive, rather than proactive.

CULTURE/UPBRINGING

America, as well as some other countries, emphasizes individual rights, independence, rugged individualism, and the like, while other cultures might emphasize family, tribe, or community. The latter is a more collectivist culture and more likely to be aware of the environment or the system within which people operate, while the former is more likely to focus on the individual and their behavior. In collectivistic cultures, individuals are a part of their group identity, a part of the family, tribe, or system, and the notion of a separate, autonomous self is highly unlikely. A collectivist culture has an easier time seeing the system as an influencer of human behavior than an individualistic culture.

It is much easier to assign causation to an individual and his or her behaviors than it is to discover all the system influences upon an individual. Our upbringing has a strong effect on our thinking patterns and how we perceive the world around us. Being able to see, think about, or discuss issues that we have never seen, thought about, or discussed is very difficult for most of us.

It's like asking individuals to identify aspects of themselves they're unaware of, a daunting task indeed. Those from individualistic cultures often view the individual as the root cause of issues, while individuals from collectivist cultures tend to first consider systemic factors before attributing blame to individuals.

GROUP-THINK

If the leader is highly autocratic, if the senior management team is homogenous, if there is little trust, or high fear, dominant personalities, or disengaged individuals, then these are some of the conditions that make it easy for groupthink to occur. It takes a brave and confident person to step up and go against the majority opinion. All too often we have seen the boss give a suggestion and everyone in the meeting took it as an order and went along with it.

Group-think does not lend itself well to system thinking, which often requires looking at organizational life and individual behavior from a larger interconnected perspective. The value of diversity of thought is that it leads to more creativity and provides better decision making. It does, however, take more time to hear the different opinions.

CHANGING PRIORITIES

What seems like a good idea this month may not look as attractive several months later and is probably relative to what are the immediate and critical needs facing you this week. So even though the executive team initially supported the change initiative and were all realistic in the amount of time and support such a project will need, months later when there are other critical needs, their support can easily wane.

Projects that are put on hold seldom regain the same level of commitment and momentum upon resumption. Typically, they gradually lose traction and fade away quietly, often resulting in their eventual abandonment.

Yet in today's world, changing priorities are more the norm rather than the exception and should be planned for and built into the change management project and openly discussed.

FADS/THEORY OF THE MOMENT

By definition, a fad is a temporary fashion or manner of conduct. Could a fad be a steppingstone to a higher level of performance, or the beginning of a new way of thinking or doing, or introduce new ideas to the organization? Could a fad be nothing more than an ephemeral idea (bell-bottom polyester leisure suits)? The answer to both questions is yes. In the business community, if you have been around any length of time, you probably have been through many fads such as Theory X & Y, self-directed work teams, quality circles, Just in time, lean manufacturing, Deming's 14 points, Malcolm Baldrige award, servant leadership, transformational leadership, inverse pyramid, values based leadership, In search of excellence - customer service programs, 7 Habit of highly effective people workshops, management and supervisory training, and the list goes on.

To be clear, all of these programs made a contribution, but only a few of them appear to have endured the test of time. Why do organizations always seem to be looking for the next big thing, the magic elixir? Is it because the environment changes and the theorists and pundits are merely responding to environmental changes and coming up with new and improved ways to handle those changes? Or could it be that the organization did not get the hoped-for results from that initiative so they moved on to see if they can get it from the next commercial initiative?

HOW DO YOU KNOW IF IT IS A FAD?

Fads tend to focus on the people, while real change initiatives tend to focus on system integration/change. Fads tend to be more motivational, while change initiatives tend to focus on either problem solving or productivity. Fads have a universality (one size fits all), while change initiatives are far more sensitive to cultural and organizational differences. Fads tend to gain credibility by the reputation and status of their proponents while real change initiatives gain credibility through verifiable results. Fads usually come from outside the organization, while real change often originates within the organization. Fads often are simplistic while real change is complex and systemic. **Fads make an impact; change makes a difference.**

Fads are often used as a quick and ready solution to complex organizational issues whereas change initiatives often evolve and focus on the root cause. Fads are often implemented quickly and applied to everyone, while change initiatives take considerably more time and maybe more focused. Fads are often prescriptive, telling the organization what needs to be done, while change initiatives are more of a discovery process that unfolds. Regardless, a fad only becomes a fad when the organization stops supporting the current initiative and moves on to the next one.

Does your organization perceive the implementation of the initiative as merely a program, an event, a training and development effort, or a short-term contract? Or does it view the initiative as an intrinsic part of its identity, embodying the "new them," aligned with its mission and values? How many resources has the organization dedicated to this new initiative, and is there a specified time limit for its execution? Furthermore, what is the driving force behind this change?

Initiatives perceived as short-term endeavors, or those operating on limited budgets, or lacking full leadership endorsement, often prove to be fleeting fads. Such initiatives tend to experience rapid ascension but ultimately fade away once the initial novelty diminishes.

Fads are often events, programs, new leadership methods, or the latest and greatest approach to whatever, but rarely integrated into the mission or purpose of the organization and supported by the core systems within an organization. For instance, if you adopt a new leadership approach what needs to change in HR, performance criteria, discipline procedures? What needs to change in finance, incentives, and bonuses? Fads have their place, but to maximize your value from a fad you need to transition it to a trend and integrate it into the organizational systems.

Currently, there are many programs being championed as the latest and greatest. Both the workforce and the environment are pushing corporations to be greener, have zero carbon footprints, install social justice programs, DEI programs, ethical marketing, support charitable causes, and, work from home programs or at least hybrid work schedules. Are these fads or harbingers of the future? Time will give us the answer.

One other measurement might be financial. If the organization were to experience a severe financial crisis, would these programs remain or be cut? Another is the number of resources dedicated to ensuring successful implementation. As noted by Dr. William Rothwell, an organization is serious about organizational change, they will dedicate resources such as budget, office space, and assistants. If the resources necessary for an initiative are lacking, it is likely to be deemed a fad. Additionally, if the proposed solution is simplistic and unlikely to bring about sustainable change, it is also indicative of a fad.[4]

INSTALLATION VS. INTEGRATION

Another way to test if a program is a fad or not is to assess if a program is more of an event rather than a process and if a program is a one-and-done or an ongoing effort. Are policies and practices being developed in support of this new initiative, is HR on board, does the initiative have total senior

---

[4] Conversation with Dr. William Rothwell, January 2024.

leadership support, is the program seen by the employees as a long-term project or flavor of the month?

In the past, numerous fads have emerged, and there's no indication that this trend will cease in the future. Fads persist because they're alluring, captivating, and often require less investment of both cost and effort compared to genuine organizational change. They tend to promote the latest ideologies, promising effortless solutions and enticing visions of success.

There are two main elements that make a program or concept a fad. Sometimes it is the product or service itself, i.e., pet rocks, Ouija boards, bell bottom leisure suits, water beds, beanie babies, management by wandering around, managerial grid, reengineering, delayering, etc. At other times it is the way the product or service is implemented. A new concept that is used as a quick solution to an ingrained organizational problem will likely fail and be considered a fad. A new concept that is assessed as to what it will and will not do for the organization and what needs to take place to maximize this new product or service, will likely be implemented with greater care and thought and become more of a trend than a fad. Executives and managers that look for shortcuts, roll the program out with a lot of fanfare and catchy phrases, talk, but do not model, ignore employee feedback, and only look for confirmation bias, all this will likely turn the innovation or idea into a fad.

The success of a program in one organization does not guarantee its success in another. Each organization operates within its unique context, facing distinct challenges, resources, and culture. What works well in one setting may not necessarily yield the same results elsewhere. For example, in one company, they use the Malcolm Baldrige format to improve organizational performance. Each manager receives training in the form and assesses their own department, then a group of those managers plus several senior managers use the information to make organizational improvements over a 12-month period forming tiger teams to address any shortcomings. In another company, they use the same Malcolm Baldrige form and assess every division, give the managers the results, and simply say improve your division with little to no follow-up. The Malcolm Baldrige approach may serve as a long-term tool for one company, while for another, it may be perceived as a passing fad. The difference lies in how it is understood, embraced, and executed by senior leaders within each organization. Any program with fad-like characteristics has the potential to become more robust through thorough vetting and integration into the organization's policies, practices, values, and strategic framework.

The following chart may be helpful in determining fads from transformation activities.

Trend	**Fad**
Process	Program
Ongoing	Event
Integrated into organization	Stand-alone
Quiet approach	Popular, in-vogue
Developed internally	Developed externally
Longevity, been around a while	Latest, greatest, and new

The following cases illustrate how fads emerge in organizations.

Case Example: Clair

Clair, an internal OD specialist, received a call from a division head wanting to provide skills training (Building Positive Relationships through Effective Communication Strategies) to one department in six locations worldwide and wanted Clair to review the curriculum to ensure sound accuracy and the accomplishment of the learning objectives stated in the design. Clair met with the division chief, and it was clear that there were a lot of unanswered questions. The division chief did not know if the same problems that he described in one location were present in all locations, that's not all, if the locations were even aware that they might receive training, did the employees want/request the training and the list of unknowns goes on. Clair thought that there were too many red flags to proceed.

The division chief also said that it must be accomplished in the next five months by the end of the fiscal year because the funds were allocated for only this year. The division chief was pushing hard to get this accomplished as they had already picked a vendor and thought the course they were providing was excellent. After several more attempts at delaying the start date to collect more data, interviewing the employees, and checking with other divisions, the mandate came down, implement this program or stand down from the assignment.

Clair knew this was going to be a waste of time and thought seriously about resigning from the assignment. Frankly, this was going against her values, wasting the company's time and money, punishing the employees, and not addressing the root cause, which was still unknown. She was not sure she wanted to work for a company that was as dictatorial as the division chief was. To further complicate matters, Clair was not sure the course was that well-constructed. The content seemed ok, but the delivery seemed more like death by PowerPoint rather than participants' involvement in the workshop. Clair also thought that maybe she was the one who was wrong and that she needed to be open to that possibility. She called all six divisions and asked them if they knew about the program and what they thought about it. As she predicted, she found a mixed response with two groups supporting the program (both friends of the division chief), two that were in a kind of wait-and-see mode, and two that did not think that training was what was needed in their division.

Armed with this data, Clair approached one of the overseas groups (Asian Pacific) to conduct a pilot program and provide an honest evaluation. She hoped that their feedback would offer valuable insights for all other regions. Despite initial hesitance, the group graciously agreed to participate.

Clair scheduled the sessions with all six groups but said it was tentative and was going to be based on the evaluation from the first course and their input. She was involving those who would be affected. A good OD practice for anyone. Furthermore, she was willing to explore the given solution (a training program) without ever knowing the root cause. She did ask the instructor to take thirty minutes from the program and invite the participants to talk about their issues as a part of the program and he agreed (again, involving those most affected by the program).

What came back from the first course surprised her. It was not the participants, nor the Asian department chief, but the instructor who came back and said that the course was not culturally appropriate and did not really address their needs and if it was going to be effective it needed to be tailored to each group. Armed with this information, Clair went to the division chief to report the training contractor information (he was present at the meeting as well) and Clair finally convinced the division chief to put a strategic pause (another OD technique) on the project while she did a discovery process (root cause analysis) from all six groups. This was going to be a brief survey to keep the project on track. He agreed.

Clair then did a combination of five interviews per department telephonically and an electronic survey of twenty individuals throughout each department. She accomplished this in two weeks and the report was ready by the third week. What came back was a list of concerns/problems, some costing the company significant loss of customers and revenue that would not in any way be resolved by any training program. Their source of frustration was the inability to serve their customers because of too many restrictive rules, policies, and mandates from their bosses. The bosses were also frustrated because many of their mandates came from one person at headquarters who was an extreme micromanager. The two departments that did not have good relations had a history of unresolved conflict that needed to be addressed.

What was initially conceived as a training solution to an unidentified issue evolved into an organizational development (OD) intervention spanning multiple levels, aimed at fostering sustainable change for both the company and its customers. In response, Clair was tasked with drafting plans for the next steps. In this pivotal moment, Clair transitioned from being an HR project manager overseeing a training program to becoming a proactive OD facilitator for the entire organization.

Later, Clair said she knew early on that what was being proposed as a solution to an organizational problem was a fad, no solution at all, and a waste of company resources. She also knew she could only push back so hard. She was also willing to accept that maybe she was wrong and like any good social scientist, try a pilot program and assess the results. In this case, the results confirmed Clair's suspicion but more important was the evidence that she needed the senior leader to see as well. Clair says that she knew she was not going to change the division manager's mind, but her goal was to get him to see what she saw and then let him make up his own mind.

Case Example: Roland

Roland had the opposite experience. His organization (a county agency) did an employee/supervisor survey, and the results were terrible, with almost everyone stating that the problem was the director of the agency, and no one trusted her. Many people did not fill out the survey because they did not believe it was going to be anonymous and felt that there would be repercussions. Unfortunately, the survey went up to the County Board and they were not pleased with this agency's report. They gave the director one year to clear it up.

The director wanted to implement various training programs which Roland knew were currently popular but would probably not change the underlying real employee concerns. The director then went on to recommend various initiatives that she read about in management magazines which again, Roland knew would probably not work in their organization because of the different conditions. Roland proposed collecting more data through interviews, focus groups, blind surveys, and pulse surveys (typical diagnostic OD tools) and all of his suggestions were turned down. He then suggested problem solving teams, to involve everyone in the effort to improve their agency, again being turned down. Roland believed that the director did not want to deal with the issue of her lack of trustworthiness or what people thought of her, so she avoided dealing with it altogether. Life went on.

At the next survey, the director said that all part-time employees and contractors would be excluded from the survey and only full-time employees above a certain level would be surveyed. These were people who had a lot to lose and subsequently gave better ratings, so the next year's report saw a vast improvement over the previous year. Also, all of the surveys went to the agency's front office before going on to be tabulated by another agency. Again, a trust issue. Roland knew that the data was skewed and that nothing improved, in fact, things were worse than the year before. For Roland, this became an ethical issue. Does he do nothing, tell the board what is going on, confront his boss, or leave the organization? Roland was also asked to implement training programs, which he knew to be fads, or go talk to people, and he knew it would do no good because they would just be addressing the symptoms, not the problems of the organization. Does he refuse the assignment?

Roland came up with the idea that he would call the program a training program to satisfy the director, but in reality, make it a venting, discussion, and problem-solving group. He became the trusted individual to whom people could vent and move on to whatever problem solving they could do. While the environment improved a little, eventually Roland left the agency because he saw there was no way to make the necessary improvements as long as the same senior leadership team was in place. Roland says that the root cause, which was obvious to everyone, was never addressed and rarely even spoken about.

Follow up – Years later, despite all of Roland's efforts, the organization continued to face challenges. Eventually, a new director assumed leadership, leading to a significant shift in the organizational culture for the better. This serves as a powerful illustration of the immense impact a senior leader can have on shaping and transforming the culture of an organization.

WHEN LEADERSHIP ENDORSES THE FAD.

When we encounter a new approach, theory, training program, or business method, it often ignites a sense of excitement within us. We become captivated by the possibilities it presents, hopeful about the positive changes it could bring, and optimistic about the potential benefits it may yield.

After all, it is new, bright, shiny, glitzy, and most importantly is just what we need. The more publicity/hype, the more we believe it to be true. We essentially buy into (believe) that this program/initiative is the one that can really help us be better. This is exactly what we need. Leadership might even experience the program themselves and become even more convinced that this will be good for the organization. The program may be a good program with all of its stated benefits. What is missing, however, is all of the elements that would transition this from a fad (flavor of the month) into a meaningful organizational trend.

- Are the organization/employees in a time and place that they could embrace a new program/initiative?
- What will we have to unlearn before we can learn something new?
- How would we implement this program and in what time frame?
- Do we have the competence among our employees to deliver this or do we employ outside resources?
- What are we trying to improve by implementing this program?
- How will we reinforce this program once it is delivered?
- What are the costs associated with the implementation?
- What in our current system, policies, and practices will need to change when we implement this program?
- How much resistance do we anticipate and how will we handle it?
- What might be some of the unintended consequences we might incur?
- What other ongoing efforts can we link with this new program?

- How long will we have to sustain this program to move it from a fad to a trend?
- How does this new program support our mission, vision, values, or strategy?
- What might cause this new program to fail or just be a fad?

The intentional practitioner who guides management through the process of considering the questions mentioned above is engaging in proactive organizational development (OD). By addressing these questions comprehensively, the practitioner ensures that the organization is well-prepared to derive maximum benefits from the implementation of initiatives.

CONCLUSION

This chapter highlights the considerations practitioners make when determining interventions for clients. There are many social, emotional, and operational elements to an organization that will determine the effectiveness of interventions. Taking time to identify and prepare for how these elements will influence a specific client will help maintain the proactivity and long-term impact we are aiming for in practicing OD.

CHAPTER 6

Cases for Reflection

The primary purpose of this chapter is to thoughtfully consider each case, discuss with others, and/or answer the introspective questions at the end of each case. These cases are not likely to show up in theoretical books or research studies but are examples of real-life situations an OD consultant may experience. They are designed to broaden the awareness of the consultant and to better prepare them for how to respond should they find themselves in the same or a similar situation. When known, the results of the cases are described in the case results appendix, and you can compare your response to what actually happened.

CASE #1: THE PRESIDENT

The newly appointed division president wanted to bring in consultants from his last division who were critical in helping the past division (comprised of 1250 employees distributed worldwide) rise to the top division in the organization. The consultants did this by implementing cultural and operational changes, executive coaching, training of supervisors and managers, implementing process and problem-solving groups (tiger teams), and involving everyone in the division in one way or another.

The initiative spanned seven to eight years, but its transformative impact was unmistakable. The division emerged as a leader within the corporation, outperforming in nearly every category measured by the company, including quality, profitability, customer service, collaborative culture, willingness to assist others, employee complaints, turnover, and more.

This new division was even larger, so the president thought that this too would be a long-term project. He wisely got his eight senior leaders who reported to him plus the on-staff organizational psychologist to form a group that would lead this organizational improvement initiative. He wanted to begin from the top down (also a wise move).

During the first meeting with the consultants, a plan was outlined for the next six months to collect data from each group, determine current employee attitudes and concerns, and primarily work with the senior leaders. The division chief spoke about how his last division was able to accomplish all that they had and wanted this group to be as successful. He thought this group was starting from a better position (i.e., less conflict), than his previous group and was hopeful that they could accomplish a lot in the next few years. He asked everyone in the room if they were on board with this initiative because he wanted to earmark the funding for the program. The accounting manager assured them that their budgets would not be taxed as the company did not have its full complement of employees all year long and the funding would move over from the excess funds left in payroll. The internal psychologist was appointed as POC for the consultants who also reported to the president.

Within three months it became obvious that the following conditions existed in the organization:

- The psychologist thought that he should be in charge and while he told the consultants he supported this initiative, he said something else to the staff.
- All the senior leaders also said they were on board, but only two really were, three were not, and three others were 'wait and see'.
- One of the groups thought they were so far ahead of the others that they did not want to wait for the others to catch up and wanted to continue their own improvement efforts at their own pace.
- The division president did not want to replace any of his senior leaders and said that as other divisions became successful, the others would also come on board, so give them some time.
- The mid-level supervisors were to be brought in after the senior staff was all on board, but the division president wanted them brought in as quickly as possible. Against better judgment, they were brought into this initiative by attending a two-day kickoff program and while the reception was mixed, they wanted the employees to be brought in right away as well.
- Also, against better judgements, employees were brought in and their level of resistance to any new program (they called it the flavor of the month) was high.

At this point, we were nine months into the first year with a lot of effort expended and little results to show for it. It is quite possible that the project will fail because all the senior leaders are not on board, nor are all the managers.

QUESTIONS

1. What is your initial reaction to this situation? Write it down.
2. What concepts, models, or theories does this case demonstrate?
3. What approach would you use with this organization?
4. What organizational (system) influences might be present?
5. What people issues might need to be addressed?
6. What would be your main recommendations?
7. What would be your first steps?
8. What are the critical issues?
9. Which of your strengths might be a good match for this client?
10. What positive and negative reactions do you have to this case? Using yourself as a barometer, what does that tell you about this organization?
11. How might your initial reactions affect your recommendations/consulting?
12. Would you continue on, or would you take a strategic pause, and if so, to do what?
13. Would you have a conversation with the psychologist, the director or other people?

CASE #2: SINCERE ABOUT CHANGE

The success story of a small, private biotech laboratory, boasting fewer than 300 employees, is noteworthy. Leveraging exclusive products unavailable elsewhere in the marketplace, the laboratory achieved remarkable success, both in terms of market recognition and financial prosperity. The founder was still running the company and he had a very autocratic way about him but could also be benign. If he liked you, you were in his good graces and he took care of you (golden handcuffs) and if he did not like you, you were just there. His orientation was a numbers person, a task person, but not a people person. He left the people's issues to the HR director.

The company was growing, and while they still had space in their current building, he purchased the building across the street which he totally gutted for remodeling (offices and labs), and another plot of land contiguous to the other side of his property for an employees' parking garage as there was limited street parking. He was managing these development/remodeling projects along with running the company. He was quite busy, and it was hard to get time with him. A significant red light[5].

You are an independent consultant with your own boutique consulting firm and this client was just recommended to you by another larger consulting firm that has used you in the past. They said the project was too small for them (only three days of training) and felt you were a good fit. The HR director called you and asked you to arrange a meeting. She met with you to outline the training she would like you to apply. As you articulated to her, the impact that this training would have on those who undergo it and those who did not, might cause some morale problems and relationship issues, especially around common

---

[5] Red lights discussed in "OD for the Accidental Practitioner," Koehler 2022.

approaches, communications, and the like. She concurred with your proposal, and as a result, the program expanded from three days of training to three sessions of three days each. This transformation elevated the project significantly, encompassing not only the development and preparation time but also the delivery of the program itself.

As you delivered the programs, you gained a lot of information from the participants that told you much more was going on here. At the end of the three training sessions, you were asked again by the HR director for your next recommendations. You gave them a nine-month plan that involved a lot of problem-solving groups and more diagnostic information gathering. They accepted your entire plan, which was now worth over $125,000, a very decent sum. They wanted you to do the work as you had gained the trust of the employees, and the HR director really liked you. This situation posed a challenge for you, particularly because she was cited multiple times as a significant issue herself. Concerns included discussing confidential matters with others when inappropriate and frequently adopting a harsh tone towards her employees, among other issues.

You started the project and many of the managers said that this would not succeed because of the founder being such a task master and number person. That this effort was doomed to fail no matter how much money they threw at it because the only reason you were hired was because the HR director liked you, and also, she and the president were intimate with one another. The president was merely letting the HR director have her way, but nothing really was going to change in the long run.

THOUGHTS

What do you do? This is a lot of money for you and not much else is on the horizon for you. Do you keep the project going and wait and see what happens, stop the project now, confront the president, or something else? What actions, if any, do you take with the HR director? Maybe the project would succeed, and it is the negative attitudes of certain employees that need to change.

QUESTIONS

1. What is your initial reaction to this situation? Write it down.
2. What concepts, models, or theories does this case demonstrate?
3. What approach would you use with this organization?
4. What organizational (system) influences might be present?
5. What people issues might need to be addressed?
6. What would be your main recommendations?
7. What would be your first steps?
8. What are the critical issues?
9. Which of your strengths might be a good match for this client?
10. What positive and negative reactions do you have to this case? Using yourself as a barometer, what does that tell you about this organization?
11. How might your initial reactions affect your recommendations/consulting?

CASE #3: NEW PLANT MANAGER

A large manufacturing firm, boasting 2400 employees in this single plant, has appointed a new plant manager with extensive manufacturing expertise and a stellar reputation. This plant manager reports to the director of operations, who expressed that the appointment was made to alleviate some of the day-to-day challenges from his desk. This strategic move enables the director of operations to concentrate on overarching strategic matters.

On his first day at the plant, it became clear to the new plant manager that there was no structure because everyone in the plant would come to him and ask him what to do. Hardly anyone went to their supervisor and many people did not even know they had a supervisor or who it was. This plant ran about 600 people per shift and there were three shifts seven days a week, so scheduling was a bit of a problem. In addition to the lack of structure, the plant manager discovered that if employees were dissatisfied with his decisions, they would circumvent him and seek the opinion of his superior, the operations director. Alternatively, they would approach him with statements like, "The PM wants to do this. Do you agree?" In many instances, the operations manager made decisions contrary to those of the plant manager, thereby undermining his authority.

The operations manager turned out to be a severe micromanager working 60 - 80 hours per week, including weekends, which is why he had all of the day-to-day decisions on his desk. He trained them that way, and furthermore, did not think of himself as a micromanager and was unaware of how his behavior affected others. He expected all of his managers, especially the plant manager, to work on weekends as well. He had been this way for the past 40 years and was now 60 years old and not likely going to change. He held the belief that the plant would collapse without his constant presence and effort, leading him to invest long hours to sustain operations. Additionally, he adopted an autocratic leadership style, insisting on his decisions without room for dissent or alternative perspectives.

In addition, the plant manager discovered dozens and dozens of other problems such as staff lying to one another, cheating on their timecards, overcrowded space, no parking for employees, employees sleeping on the job, dating one another, physically damaging property, nepotism, quality issues, high wastage of product, poor customer service, and other assorted issues.

QUESTIONS

1. What is your initial reaction to this situation? Write it down.
2. What concepts, models, or theories does this case demonstrate?
3. What approach would you use with this organization?
4. What organizational (system) influences might be present?
5. What people issues might need to be addressed?
6. What would be your main recommendations?
7. What would be your first steps?
8. What are the critical issues?
9. Which of your strengths might be a good match for this client?

10. What positive and negative reactions do you have to this case? Using yourself as a barometer, what does that tell you about this organization?
11. How might your initial reactions affect your recommendations/consulting?

CASE #4: DO AS I SAY?

You have been hired by an organization of about 1800 employees to deliver a very specific program to one of their departments. A team building program that will focus on developing common goals for this newly formed department of twenty-one people and develop a set of departmental values in line with corporate values. You have been thinking of using the four stages Tuckman model as a basis for this workshop, adding on the values piece toward the end of this two-day event. You have also arranged for two follow-up sessions two weeks apart after the initial workshop. There is a shared understanding that this engagement is temporary, and the goal is for the newly formed department to become self-sufficient within a relatively brief timeframe. The teambuilding workshop was to be performed on-site in the organization's large conference room which was nicely decorated and had a small kitchenette for refreshments.

During the teambuilding event, information surfaces in various discussions that it will be difficult to be a team when upper management does not model that behavior at all, in fact, they are quite contentious and frequently at odds with one another. They openly show their disdain for one another and with the rest of the organization. You were hired by the HR director for this team building program, so you have no real exposure to the senior team. Every time they discuss processes and practices that make a good team, inevitably someone will refer to the senior team and their lack of using these traits. Furthermore, when they begin to discuss their values, and how they will treat one another, it again comes up that senior management does not live by the corporate values. There are the stated values posted on the lobby walls, and then there are the real values, how they really operate on a day-to-day basis, and they are not the same. They feel the company is duplicitous in posting their values.

Additionally, you frequently overhear an individual outside the conference room yelling and cursing, creating what you believe to be a hostile work environment. In your assessment, this behavior likely violates Title VII of the Civil Rights Act and various state laws. To your dismay, you discover that the individual is a supervisor in another department. You are convinced that this situation is a lawsuit waiting to happen. You are now aware of several major issues for this organization, all that may affect the outcome of your work with this team, and none of which are in your current contract to deal with.

THOUGHTS

- Do you only deal with the team, or do you include the senior managers, the HR director, your POC, and the person in the hallway? How do you handle these issues?
- If you proceed with your team building program, in what ways will your efforts help the organization and hurt the organization?
- Is your team building program doomed to fail because of the senior managers? Or, in what ways might it be successful?

QUESTIONS

1. What is your initial reaction to this situation? Write it down.
2. What concepts, models, or theories does this case demonstrate?
3. What approach would you use with this organization?
4. What organizational (system) influences might be present?
5. What people issues might need to be addressed?
6. What would be your main recommendations?
7. What would be your first steps?
8. What are the critical issues?
9. Which of your strengths might be a good match for this client?
10. What positive and negative reactions do you have to this case? Using yourself as a barometer, what does that tell you about this organization?
11. How might your initial reactions affect your recommendations/consulting?

CASE # 5: TRUST

You are an internal OD consultant for a division of an organization and are a member of the senior staff of the division. You report to the division director, whose trustworthiness you question, as you perceive her to be two-faced and deeply entrenched in office politics. You believe her to be devious and will say anything to look good to her boss. Her boss is the operations manager, and the operations manager reports to the CEO of the entire organization. The operations manager has a reputation for being a good person, with good intent, but is unwilling to fire anyone and always willing to give people a second chance. Despite individuals being caught engaging in illegal activities, she is known to offer them second chances. However, you recognize that even if she receives negative feedback about your director, she is unlikely to take action for two reasons: she lacks a viable replacement, and she refrains from removing staff members without cause. Therefore, lodging complaints about the division director's behavior to her superior would likely yield no results.

In the meantime, the lack of trust by everyone in your director is demoralizing the organization and causing some people to leave and others to just do the minimum, collect their paycheck, and go home. While everyone talks about it, most staff have no hope that anything will be done and when people do complain up to headquarters, nothing of substance really happens.

One individual remarked, "If it wasn't for the low morale, there would be none at all." Despite your willingness to engage with all groups within the division, you harbor doubts about the efficacy of utilizing your skills with senior leaders as long as the current director remains in power.

THOUGHTS

- How do you handle an organization with low trust?
- What do you do when the senior leaders are the problem?
- How candidly are you able to speak to the senior leaders?
- What do you do in the absence of any good options?

QUESTIONS

1. What is your initial reaction to this situation? Write it down.
2. What concepts, models, or theories does this case demonstrate?
3. What approach would you use with this organization?
4. What organizational (system) influences might be present?
5. What people issues might need to be addressed?
6. What would be your main recommendations?
7. What would be your first steps?
8. What are the critical issues?
9. Which of your strengths might be a good match for this client?
10. What positive and negative reactions do you have to this case? Using yourself as a barometer, what does that tell you about this organization?
11. How might your initial reactions affect your recommendations/consulting?

CASE #6: ORGANIZATIONAL DESIGN

You have been recruited by a prominent retail chain with 111 stores spread across 49 states, organized into five regions. Each region is overseen by its own President, who reports directly to the Senior Operations Director. You have been asked to review their current organizational structure, especially how the regions are organized, and come up with a better organizational design and new organization chart. During a visit to one of the stores to interview management, you learn that this store has a high theft rate. Store security says most of the theft comes from shoplifters, but the company has inconsistent enforcement and gives you this example. Recently a thirteen-year-old boy was charged with shoplifting and released to his parents after taking a package of batteries for his electronic devices, while an 84-year-old lady was let go without being charged after taking off-the-shelf medicine she could not afford. In addition, quite a few employees help themselves with things like soda pop or cut open a bag of food so they can say it was damaged and then eat it. The store seems to turn a blind eye to these types of activities, but it all adds up.

Upon requesting theft reports from stores with high theft rates, and collaborating with HR, it becomes evident that these same stores also exhibit high employee turnover and complaint rates. This observation suggests a potential positive correlation between poor leadership and elevated theft incidents. Surprisingly, no correlation is found between higher theft rates and specific regions. Additionally, you discover that the stores that have high theft and turnover rates were high-performing stores just a year or two ago. The data is very inconsistent and there does not appear to be any clear trends or correlations. You are concerned that the internal issues are more behavioral, and any new design may not solve these issues and may even encourage more unintended consequences. Taking on more diagnostic work will likely put you over budget and your deliverable (a new org design) will likely not be met without additional funding.

THOUGHTS

Do you proceed with the new design, taking into consideration all that you know, or put the design on hold until you get to the root cause of the problems?

- Do you ignore the internal issues and create the best design possible for this organization? Other?

QUESTIONS

1. What is your initial reaction to this situation? Write it down.
2. What concepts, models, or theories does this case demonstrate?
3. What approach would you use with this organization?
4. What organizational (system) influences might be present?
5. What people issues might need to be addressed?
6. What would be your main recommendations?
7. What would be your first steps?
8. What are the critical issues?
9. Which of your strengths might be a good match for this client?
10. What positive and negative reactions do you have to this case? Using yourself as a barometer, what does that tell you about this organization?
11. How might your initial reactions affect your recommendations/consulting?

Case #7: Petty Cash

A large trucking firm has hired you to review their morning operations and report back on how they could be more efficient and organized. Every morning, the scene unfolds with a flurry of chaos as truckers question their routes, encounter shortages on their loads, and request petty cash from the dispatcher for minor truck maintenance items such as lights, wipers, windshield washer fluid, brake fluid, and more.

After just two days of observing you have several recommendations for management:

1. Stagger start times so that not everyone is arriving at the same time.
2. All incorrect loads should go to one person to verify and correct.
3. Petty cash should be dispensed by an administrative person, not the dispatcher.
4. Give each driver "X" amount of money per week to purchase anything needed for their trucks (must have receipts) and they only reconcile their account once every two weeks or month.

The company strongly resisted the last suggestion, believing that their minor parts costs would go through the roof, but after much discussion (sometimes heated), they decided on $20.00 per week per driver and would pilot this for two months. All your suggestions were implemented, and the operations became considerably smoother. Contrary to their belief that the costs for truck parts would escalate, the reality was quite the opposite: their parts costs significantly decreased. Suddenly, the need for truck parts appeared to diminish substantially.

THOUGHTS

- What could explain the decrease in spending for truck parts?

QUESTIONS

1. What is your initial reaction to this situation? Write it down.
2. What concepts, models, or theories does this case demonstrate?
3. What approach would you use with this organization?
4. What organizational (system) influences might be present?
5. What people issues might need to be addressed?
6. What would be your main recommendations?
7. What would be your first steps?
8. What are the critical issues?
9. Which of your strengths might be a good match for this client?
10. What positive and negative reactions do you have to this case? Using yourself as a barometer, what does that tell you about this organization?
11. How might your initial reactions affect your recommendations/consulting?

CASE #8: UNAWARE

Jim, a creative artist and sole proprietor of a small business, and an acquaintance, has asked for your help in growing his business. He barely gets by, but always seems to do just that. He is competent at attracting new customers through his creative endeavors but seems to have a difficult time keeping his customers and getting repeat business. A talkative and friendly sort, he is always willing to spend time chatting with folks. Jim is unaware that most of his chatting is complaining about almost anything, and he is highly negative and slightly aggressive in his tone of voice. He also tends to put others down by calling them names like stupid, incompetent, and Darwin's mistake.

He acknowledges the transient nature of relationships in his life, having experienced divorce, loss of previous friendships, and difficulty retaining customers. Despite these challenges, he perceives himself as a kind-hearted individual. When confronted with feedback about his negativity, he is taken aback and unaware of his negative demeanor. To him, that is just the way he talks. Nothing out of the ordinary for him. When being critical, he sees himself as realistic, or as someone who tends to see problems that others miss. He tends to bring everyone around him down. Even if he does hear feedback about his negativity, he is back at it again in five minutes.

THOUGHTS

- Who are the negative people in your organization?
- How do they affect the environment/others?
- How do you interact with them?
- What or who supports their negativity?
- What would it take to change their negativity or way of thinking?

QUESTIONS

1. What is your initial reaction to this situation? Write it down.
2. What concepts, models, or theories does this case demonstrate?
3. What approach would you use with this organization?
4. What organizational (system) influences might be present?
5. What people issues might need to be addressed?
6. What would be your main recommendations?
7. What would be your first steps?
8. What are the critical issues?
9. Which of your strengths might be a good match for this client?
10. What positive and negative reactions do you have to this case? Using yourself as a barometer, what does that tell you about this organization?
11. How might your initial reactions affect your recommendations/consulting?

CASE #9: MEGA SYSTEM

A government hospital system has 171 medical centers and 1113 outpatient clinics throughout the world. As you can imagine, each location has its own unique culture and idiosyncrasies. Similarly, within a medical center, each department will also possess its distinct culture and dynamics. This is quite a complex system, and add to that, the cultural differences from overseas locations and it becomes even more complex. You have been asked by senior management to help change the culture, make it more positive, more patient-oriented, less wait time, higher employee morale, and other factors. This is your full-time job, and you have a staff of 50 professional OD consultants/psychologists.

THOUGHTS

- Is the goal obtainable?
- Do you work on changing the culture as requested or work on the people or system?

QUESTIONS

1. What is your initial reaction to this situation? Write it down.
2. What concepts, models, or theories does this case demonstrate?
3. What approach would you use with this organization?
4. What organizational (system) influences might be present?
5. What people issues might need to be addressed?
6. What would be your main recommendations?
7. What would be your first steps?
8. What are the critical issues?
9. Which of your strengths might be a good match for this client?
10. What positive and negative reactions do you have to this case? Using yourself as a barometer, what does that tell you about this organization?
11. How might your initial reactions affect your recommendations/consulting?

CASE #10: DISTANCE FROM HEADQUARTERS

As an external consultant, you operate with a team consisting of three full-time employees and six part-time or contractual workers. You have been hired to deliver a specific training program to eight locations of this organization scattered all over the country. This is a three-day training program focused on enhancing interpersonal relationships, a workshop that you have facilitated at least fifteen times in the past and are highly experienced with. Adhering to principles of adult education, you are well-versed in creating an optimal learning environment. In preparation, you provide the organization with a detailed outline of your classroom seating arrangement and specific requirements. In return, the organization furnishes you with the names and contact details of your designated points of contact at each location. Additionally, they receive a copy of your requirements, which include the following:

- Maximum number of participants per class.
- Seating arrangements.
- Up front speakers table, supply table, computer, projector (for PowerPoint slides), speaker's chair, flip charts (when they were popular).
- Room with heating and lighting controls, windows for outside lighting but with shades or blinds for blocking out intense sunlight.
- Break times with snacks, coffee, tea, and juice.
- Workbook reproduction, classroom handouts, and materials.
- Quiet environment.
- Introduction by a senior staff member.

The day arrived for the first program at headquarters, and everything proceeded remarkably smoothly, culminating in excellent reviews at the conclusion of the session. Senior management was pleased and complimented you and your colleagues. The second program had a few bumps in the preparation and the room was not quite as requested, but with a simple moving of the tables and chairs it was good to go. The program had more naysayers in it and the evaluations were slightly more negative, but overall, still very good.

Well, the program went downhill from there, with each succeeding location worse and worse until finally at one location, nothing was done in preparation for the program, nothing was set up, materials could not be found, it was not certain the invite went out and more importantly, no one cared. You had two programs left to deliver and, in an effort, to avoid even worse programs, you decided to give the senior leader feedback on how the program was going, hoping that they could help salvage the last two programs.

At the meeting with senior leaders, you provided them with candid feedback indicating that the further geographically from headquarters, there seemed to be less and less interest in the program and less and less responsibility to see that it was a good program. Many of the locations were negative about this program, thinking that this was just something that headquarters thought up and was really interfering with their workload. You further described how negative some people were toward any training, toward you and your colleagues, and toward their own bosses and organization.

Senior management patiently listened to your report and when you were finished you asked them for their reaction to all that you said. They looked at you and said, "That is pretty much what we expected." They went on further to say that this is pretty much what the culture has been like for the last five plus years. Astonishingly you asked, "Why haven't you addressed or fixed this?" and they answered back, "Frankly we don't know how, that was what we were hoping your class would do."

THOUGHTS

- Where do you go from here?
- Do you keep on with the remaining training programs or use those funds elsewhere?

QUESTIONS

1. What is your initial reaction to this situation? Write it down.
2. What concepts, models, or theories does this case demonstrate?
3. What approach would you use with this organization?
4. What organizational (system) influences might be present?
5. What people issues might need to be addressed?
6. What would be your main recommendations?
7. What would be your first steps?
8. What are the critical issues?
9. Which of your strengths might be a good match for this client?

10. What positive and negative reactions do you have to this case? Using yourself as a barometer, what does that tell you about this organization?
11. How might your initial reactions affect your recommendations/consulting?

CASE #11: PEOPLE OR SYSTEM

You have been hired and tasked with resolving a conflict within an office comprising approximately 80 individuals. The director, nearing retirement, is characterized as a kind-hearted individual who perceives himself as supportive to all employees. He refrains from speaking negatively about anyone, avoids disciplinary actions or terminations, and prefers informal conversations as needed. Despite his positive outlook on the organization, all of his senior staff members harbor a strong aversion towards him, bordering on hatred.

There are two lawyers who think that because of their background, they are more educated than the rest of the senior leaders and smarter and better suited for the job. There are two others who have been there for fifteen-plus years and believe that they are better suited for the job and run their respective departments better than anyone else and know more than anyone else. Then there are two people who tend to stay out of the hassle and just keep to themselves and try to get the work done. One teleworks and rarely ever comes into the workplace to avoid the atmosphere. This is the senior leadership team. They occasionally call on the HR guy for help and he is quite in tune with what is going on, and often has good advice, but also stays out of the fray as much as possible and is going to a new position elsewhere in the organization within five months.

Furthermore, tension permeates the office as employees have naturally aligned themselves with their respective managers, exacerbating the existing conflict. Compounding the situation is the presence of a contentious union representative, who habitually adopts a confrontational tone, harbors deep-seated animosity towards management, and harbors distrust towards management decisions. This representative routinely files labor grievances with the board, even garnering weariness from her own board members.

Customer service is very inconsistent and quite dependent on who you talk to and what advice you are given. Additionally, there is a significant number of contract workers who do the same work as employees but without the same benefits and job security, causing dissension among all employees.

QUESTIONS

1. What is your initial reaction to this situation? Write it down.
2. What concepts, models, or theories does this case demonstrate?
3. What approach would you use with this organization?
4. What organizational (system) influences might be present?
5. What people issues might need to be addressed?
6. What would be your main recommendations?
7. What would be your first steps?
8. What are the critical issues?

9. Which of your strengths might be a good match for this client?

10. What positive and negative reactions do you have to this case? Using yourself as a barometer, what does that tell you about this organization?

11. How might your initial reactions affect your recommendations/consulting?

CASE #12: LONG MEETING

A military base had several contract businesses on base, food service, gas station, car wash, tailors, barbers, etc. In addition, they had the normal BX and Commissary. There were several issues that needed to be ironed out regarding who did what. All involved parties demanded a seat at the table, so you had base administration, housing, legal, unions (there were several), private sector representatives, DCA representatives, and others. This was a rather large meeting of thirty-plus people at each meeting. The meetings last for two hours once a month. They conducted nine to ten meetings per year, occasionally missing a month for summer vacations, Christmas holidays, etc. Five years later, they were still meeting with no significant decisions made. The meeting lacked permanent facilitators, a defined decision-making process, clear agendas, and a structured conflict resolution mechanism. Consequently, conflicts arose frequently, compounded by the absence of established norms, rules, or shared values within the group. The only unifying objective was to reconcile differences and devise a mutually satisfactory plan for moving forward.

QUESTIONS

1. What is your initial reaction to this situation? Write it down.
2. What concepts, models, or theories does this case demonstrate?
3. What approach would you use with this organization?
4. What organizational (system) influences might be present?
5. What people issues might need to be addressed?
6. What would be your main recommendations?
7. What would be your first steps?
8. What are the critical issues?
9. Which of your strengths might be a good match for this client?
10. What positive and negative reactions do you have to this case? Using yourself as a barometer, what does that tell you about this organization?
11. How might your initial reactions affect your recommendations/consulting?

CASE #13: MERGER MANIA

Two founding CEOs of local companies had grown their respective organizations to 2000-3000 employees each and both had a national and growing international presence. Company A had outstanding products with an equally outstanding reputation envied by company B. Company B had a national distribution system with many brick-and-mortar locations envied by company A. Each company was about ten to fifteen years old and both founders were still actively running their respective organizations. Both companies had their headquarters in the same city. The owners decided to merge their respective companies. Most, maybe all, mergers take more time, require more resources, cost more, and have more problems than anticipated and this merger was no exception.

After the merger was legally formalized the following issues emerged, some anticipated, some not.

- Computer systems did not talk with one another.
- Different financial accounting methods.
- Many more locations with competing stores than they thought.
- Sales systems were completely different with one company having protected geographical areas and the other company with no boundaries.
- Different bonus programs.
- Company A sold services and Company B sold products. They did not know how, nor did they want, to sell each other's services or products.
- Severe distrust and jealousy among the two different staffs.
- No marketing plan after the merger announcement.
- A strong shift away from a customer focus to an internal focus.
- Many strong rumors due to the lack of or confusing communications.
- Different company policies and HR needed to produce a new employee handbook considering both organizations.
- Different cultures, one more people-centric and the other more product-oriented.
- Similar values, but different missions, and very different visions.

- Different long-range plans and strategies.
- Both companies had a strong lack of diversity within their ranks and tended to be male oriented.
- High level of dysfunction affecting customer service and sales.
- Decision to move into one new corporate headquarters, causing both organization's staff to drive 40 miles one way to the new office. The new offices are beautiful and there is some competition for who gets the nicer offices.

You are asked to help resolve these issues and smooth out the merger and are given one year to do it. There has been no discussion of resources, or budget at this point.

THOUGHTS

- Is the goal realistic?

QUESTIONS

1. What is your initial reaction to this situation? Write it down.
2. What concepts, models, or theories does this case demonstrate?
3. What approach would you use with this organization?
4. What organizational (system) influences might be present?
5. What people issues might need to be addressed?
6. What would be your main recommendations?
7. What would be your first steps?
8. What are the critical issues?

9. Which of your strengths might be a good match for this client?

10. What positive and negative reactions do you have to this case? Using yourself as a barometer, what does that tell you about this organization?

11. How might your initial reactions affect your recommendations/consulting?

CASE #14: I AM BIASED

Gloria was hired as an intern at a large corporation last summer before graduation and she did so well that the same organization offered her a full-time job upon graduation. Within a week of starting her job at the company, Gloria uncovered a disconcerting reality: several supervisors exhibited sexist and racist attitudes. What was particularly troubling was that this behavior wasn't isolated to a few individuals but rather seemed to permeate throughout the workplace. Gloria observed a prevalence of off-color jokes, innuendos, and inappropriate language, creating a hostile and uncomfortable environment.

It was so bad that within one year she quit and moved into a completely different field, manufacturing. In her new company, there were none of the previous problems. Instead, this organization had incredibly high-performance goals and employee safety rules and regulations that were ignored. The more Gloria looked around, the more she saw unsafe conditions, in the stairwell, parking lot, restrooms, cafeteria, and on the shop floor. Management was aware of these issues, but the employees could not get management to respond. It seemed that all management wanted was to meet production goals, in any way possible. Their bonuses were based on their production.

Another really great opportunity became available in yet another industry, aeronautics, and Gloria decided to take advantage of it, so she switched industries once again. To her good fortune, neither of the two previous conditions existed in this job. However, what Gloria soon discovered was that there was no real work life balance, 60-hour weeks were common, as was being available to emails and phone calls on weekends. Taking off any personal time was frowned upon and even affected several individuals' promotions. While the work was exciting and the people were good, it was overwhelming. So once again after about a year, Gloria left the organization for an even larger multinational organization and for a significant pay increase and better benefits which were highly advertised.

Within six months, Gloria discovered why the pay was so high and benefits were so good; it was because this organization was all about the money. Making money was paramount. The real mission of this organization was to make lots and lots of money. "Money matters" was the phrase many employees used to describe the mission of the organization. Senior executives were paid in the mid and upper six figures, mid-level managers were paid in the $200,000 to $300,000 range, and entry-level people in the low six figures. Greed was evident everywhere. Gloria, who saw herself as more service than money oriented, was not happy.

After almost seven years in corporate America, Gloria finally left for a much smaller nonprofit mission driven organization of thirty people. She absolutely loved her job as well as the people and the mission of the organization.

QUESTIONS

1. What is your initial reaction to this situation? Write it down.
2. What concepts, models, or theories does this case demonstrate?
3. What approach would you use with this organization/individual?
4. Based on Gloria's experience, what might be her belief/judgment about large corporations?
5. What biases for or against large corporations might she have?
6. What experiences or beliefs do you have with large corporations?
7. What biases do you have about large corporations?
8. How might your biases affect your consulting?

CHAPTER 7

Questions for Self-Reflection

The OD consultant is an instrument of change. Your very presence affects the system and all of the people you interact with. You are a model. The questions you must ask are: what are you modeling, what impact on others are you making, and how is your presence affecting the organization? However, you come with your own baggage. You take yourself and all your habits, experiences, biases, strengths, and weaknesses with you wherever you go.

Being an instrument of change transcends mere physical presence; it encompasses the way you communicate with individuals, your tone of voice, facial expressions, body language, character, personality, intelligence, emotions, motivation, enthusiasm, patience, reactions, and more. Therefore, self-awareness is crucial in navigating this role effectively.

This chapter is best used with your active involvement. This chapter will take considerable time if you answer the questions, and especially, if you discuss the questions and answers in a group. There are a mix of questions regarding yourself, others, and the organization. The questions are designed to provoke thought and introspection. The more you are aware of yourself, your preferences, biases, strengths, and weaknesses, the more strategically and deliberately you can use yourself in the service of the client organization. As your awareness of, and sensitivity to self and others increases, it is likely that your skillfulness in working with others will increase as well.

Pick a time and place where you will not be interrupted and can give sufficient time and thought to each question. You may wish to journal your answers. Some questions will be easy to answer while other questions will take more thought and time. Feel free to use these questions in any way that will benefit you or your group. For simplicity's sake, the categories of questions are arranged in three areas, awareness, people skills, and organization skills. There is no significance to the order.

These questions are not all-inclusive and only represent an introduction to introspection and self-understanding. While some questions may have short quick answers, others may require more energy and are better suited for multiple thinking sessions. These questions can be enhanced by discussions with a team of fellow consultants. The goal for the consultant is to know thyself well, to know your areas of strength and improvement. For many consultants, becoming more skillful is the result of gaining more experience. By going through this list of questions, you should be able to identify what additional skills and experiences are necessary. If an answer is not known to you, move on to the next question. Some questions may require feedback or input from others who know you.

The categories were formulated based on a review of OD and Consulting competency models, combined with insights gleaned from our hands-on experience working with diverse clients. It's important to acknowledge that these questions reflect a predominantly Western cultural perspective. Depending on your cultural background or national origin, some questions or categories may resonate more strongly than others. We encourage you to adapt the list to suit your context and share it with others who may benefit from the reflective exercise.

AWARENESS AND UNDERSTANDING OF SELF

You bring yourself everywhere, so it is critically important that you know who and what you are bringing to the client organization. What/who you like and do not like, your relationships, recommendations, how you approach work, your strengths, weaknesses, biases, and everything you do is influenced by who you are today. How you got there is influenced by your upbringing, community, education, experiences, values, etc. Knowing who others are is good, knowing yourself is both difficult and essential.

1. What do I get irritated about?
2. What am I most understanding or compassionate about?
3. What are my core values?
4. How often do I violate my core values?
5. How often do people come to me to vent or seek advice?
6. Do I see myself as a trainer, change agent, consultant, or other?
7. What do I tend to laugh at?
8. What do I tend to be judgmental about?
9. What do others say are my blind spots?
10. How well am I able to differ with or confront senior executives (speak truth to power).
11. What are my biases, likes and dislikes? Name as many as you can.
12. When am I most patient and impatient?

Beliefs

Your beliefs are your convictions or mindset about someone or something. They can be based on observations, facts, or hearsay. Beliefs are not necessarily truths or facts, just something you believe in. Beliefs often are the foundation for judgements and biases, whether true or not. This section explores some of your beliefs although you likely have many other beliefs.

1. A good style of leadership for today's organization is…
2. A good organizational design for engaged employees is…
3. High performing teams have…
4. Conflict is…
5. DEI programs are…
6. Dialogic OD is…
7. Diagnostic OD is…
8. Who do I think is more sensitive to emotions, men or women?
9. When it comes to work emotions should…
10. OD is…
11. When it comes to OD, is it better to be an (internal or external) consultant?
12. What percent of my beliefs are based on verifiable facts, what I hear from others, what I read or saw somewhere, judgments, or interpretations?

Situational Awareness

Situational awareness extends beyond mere perception and comprehension of one's environment; it encompasses the capacity to adeptly respond to varying circumstances. Consciousness of one's surroundings and the influence one exerts on others fosters sound decision-making and cultivates stronger relationships founded on empathy and understanding. In crisis situations, situational awareness saves lives.

1. I am rarely, sometimes, usually, frequently, always aware of my surroundings.
2. How much time do I spend looking at my phone while outdoors or walking?
3. How preoccupied (or deep in other thoughts) am I while driving?
4. Am I more sensitive to tone of voice, facial expressions, emotions, or behaviors?
5. How often do I get caught up in the content and not pay attention to the process of a meeting?
6. Can I tell where a meeting will likely end up after the first 10 minutes of the meeting?
7. Do I rarely, sometimes, usually, frequently, always spot potential problems before they become a problem?
8. Do I rarely, sometimes, usually, frequently, always see or observe things that other people miss?
9. Do I rarely, sometimes, usually, frequently, always see potential risks or hazards before they become a crisis?
10. Do I rarely, sometimes, usually, frequently, always see the connection between cause and effect?

ATTITUDE

Attitude encompasses one's manner, disposition, or inclination towards something or someone. While some individuals possess a pessimistic attitude, perceiving problems at every turn, others exhibit an optimistic outlook, recognizing opportunities in every situation.

1. On a scale of 1 (low) -10 (high) how positive and negative am I?
2. How do I deal with other people's negativity?
3. How often do I complain, or criticize?
4. How often am I judgmental of others?
5. What am I most positive/negative about?
6. Does the weather affect me, if so, how?
7. When things go wrong what is my typical reaction?
8. Is my self-talk mostly positive or negative?
9. Am I unhappy, neutral, or happy with my life right now?

PEOPLE SKILLS

Relationship Builder

These questions can refer to individuals as well as levels of people in the organization such as executives, senior managers, mid managers, supervisors, workforce, entry-level, etc.

1. Who do I tend to favor/like?
2. Who do I tend to stay away from or dislike?
3. What specific things do I do to improve my relationship with others?
4. Am I more task or people focused? What are the benefits or distractors of that orientation?
5. Scale of 1-10 (high) how caring am I? Your evaluation of self may differ from the evaluation from others. Asking others for feedback will reduce blind spots.
6. Scale of 1-10 how respectful am I?
7. Scale of 1-10 how compassionate am I?
8. Scale of 1-10 how trusting am I?
9. How sensitive am I to other people's emotions, scale of 1-10?

10. Describe your relationship with your boss, peers, and subordinates. Is any level more difficult than another?

EMOTIONAL COMPETENCY

Humans are emotional creatures. Most individuals cannot remember anything before the age of four to five years old, that is when your Hippocampus begins to formulate long term memories. Prior to that, we generally responded to the world emotionally, when we were cold or hungry or got hurt, we cried, when we wanted something, we became insistent. We responded to our world emotionally. We are emotional creatures that think. Being aware of your emotions is often thought of as being emotionally intelligent, but using your emotions to your benefit and the benefit of others is referred to as emotional competency.

1. Which emotion do I tend to express most easily, mad, sad, glad, or scared?
2. How sensitive, (scale 1-10), to my emotions am I?
3. How sensitive to the emotions of others am I?
4. What are my hot buttons?
5. How do I handle other people when they are angry with me?
6. Do I let people know when I am mad, sad, glad, or scared?
7. How do I handle other people when they are mad, sad, glad, or scared?
8. How often do I have emotions and am not aware of them, but other people might be?
9. How often do I use my emotions as a barometer of what is happening?

10. Rank in order from most to least the emotions you tend to express, - mad, sad, glad, or scared.

BUILDING TRUST

The phrase "without trust, there is no us" holds significant truth. Trust serves as the bedrock for all enduring and fruitful relationships. In organizational contexts, if individuals fail to trust the consultant, the consultant's effectiveness is inherently compromised. Trust is cultivated when others perceive you as reliable, consistently acting with integrity, and demonstrating competence. While some individuals may readily extend trust, others require substantial time and experience to develop trust in someone. Building trust is a gradual process, yet it can be shattered in an instant. Once trust is eroded, rebuilding it is often arduous and time-intensive, with no guarantee of restoration.

1. What behaviors do I have that tend to build trust?
2. What behaviors do I have that tend to build distrust?
3. What commitments do I tend to forget?
4. Am I on time for meetings?
5. Who do I trust and not trust and why?
6. What does my team/department/organization need to do to increase trust?
7. What can I do to help build trust within my organization?
8. How trustworthy am I (ask others)?

COMMUNICATION SKILLS

Far more than merely imparting or interchanging thoughts or opinions, communications include listening, speaking, writing, pictures, signs, nonverbals, and body language. It also includes knowledge, facts, and emotions.

Being able to both present a point of view and listen to and consider other points of view are important skills for any consultant. Being able to sway another person by your logic, facts or emotions is also a part of communication skills.

1. On a scale of 1-10 (10 high), how transparent is my organization?
2. What is the primary method for communication with employees?
3. How frequently does the organization communicate with employees?
4. On a scale of 1-10 how effective are senior leadership communication skills (average)?
5. On a scale of 1-10 how good of a listener am I?
6. What can I do to be a better communicator/listener?
7. How does my physical location(s) affect communications?
8. How does my organizational design (chart) affect communications?
9. How often do people in my organization interrupt or talk over one another?
10. How often do I interrupt or talk over others?
11. What are my most frequently displayed nonverbal clues?
12. When frustrated what is my tone of voice?

ORGANIZATION SKILLS

These questions relate to your current job/position.

1. What work do I most enjoy?
2. What work do I least enjoy?
3. What motivates me the most about work?
4. What has been one of my best accomplishments so far?
5. What skills are important for my current position?

6. What skills are important for my profession?
7. What skills do I need to improve and how will I do that?
8. What percent of time do I spend on important work and what percent on unimportant or busy work (must add up to 100%)?
9. How might I be more useful to my organization?

SYSTEMS INFLUENCE

How does the compensation and bonus structure impact employee behavior? Similarly, what influence do HR systems such as discipline, promotion, and operational rules and policies exert on employee conduct? It's crucial to recognize that all these systems play a pivotal role in shaping and potentially determining human behavior. Being able to think systemically is essential to determining the root cause.

1. What are the core systems of my organization (or ones I am working with)?
2. What problems is my organization facing and which core system influences this behavior?
3. What rules or policies do we have that are obsolete?
4. Where is the most inefficient area in our organization and what supports those results?
5. What behaviors does our compensation system influence?
6. What behaviors does our sales system influence?
7. What rules or procedures do we have regarding customer service?
8. How are mistakes treated in my organization?
9. How does my system contribute to the organizational culture?

10. What rules or policies contribute to employee engagement and disengagement?

FACILITATION

This is a critical and essential skill for all consultants. You will be in many meetings either as a participant or leader. Many meetings are poorly organized and run. Being able to move the group along and accomplish the objectives or make the meeting productive is a necessary skill for any consultant.

1. How effective are my meetings?
2. How are decisions made in my meetings?
3. What causes meetings to be a waste of time?
4. Are there people who tend to dominate meetings and why?
5. Are there people who tend to not participate and why?
6. Which type of personality is most difficult for me to handle in a meeting?
7. How effectively do I manage meeting durations? If they frequently exceed allotted timeframes, what factors contribute to this?
8. Do people attend meetings and not know why they are there?
9. Who tends to run the best meetings and what do they do differently?
10. Is there a better way to disseminate the information other than a meeting?
11. Are most of my meetings informational, decision making, or implementation oriented?
12. Which meetings could be eliminated with little to no consequence?

13. Do people multitask during meetings? Why?

14. Are most of my meetings via technology or in person?

15. When using any remote meeting platform, do people stay on camera or do they block video recording (usually to do other tasks)?

16. How would I make my meetings more effective and beneficial?

17. Do the meeting leaders plan the meeting, the room, and the material in advance or do they tend to just wing it when the meeting starts?

DIAGNOSTIC ABILITIES

This encompasses the capacity to investigate, identify, analyze, interpret, and characterize prevailing conditions, forging connections between causes and outcomes to address challenges and enhance organizational performance. It involves transcending simplistic cause-and-effect relationships and fostering trusting relationships to elicit candid feedback from individuals, even those who may harbor skepticism or with whom you have no prior acquaintance. Additionally, it entails organizing information coherently, formulating recommendations grounded in findings, and presenting them to senior leadership in a manner that facilitates comprehension, acceptance, and strategic action planning for the future.

1. What methods do I use to collect information?

2. On a scale of 1-10 (10 high) how good am I at interviewing?

3. On a scale of 1-10 how good am I at conducting focus group interviews?

4. Everything we do has a diagnostic element to it, what is a good source(s) of information for me?
5. On a scale of 1-10 how good am I at discovering root cause?
6. How much time do I spend in personal observation of other groups/teams?
7. Do I use written surveys and when?
8. Do I use ongoing pulse surveys?
9. How accurate are my interpretations and recommendations?
10. What do I do when people are hesitant to be honest with me?

BUILDING TEAM COLLABORATION

Collaboration is the mindset; cooperation is the behavior. Taking a group of individuals and transforming them into a team is not always easy. Establishing a common worthwhile goal, however, is a crucial first step. The ability to work with diverse people and change whatever individualistic behaviors and paradigms they might have to a collaborative mindset and supporting one another in search for a common goal is not always easy but is always important for team collaboration.

1. Which teams have the greatest collaboration or conflict and why?
2. Which teams seem to support one another best?
3. How comfortable am I with conflict?
4. What is the primary way I handle conflict?
5. What policies or practices encourage collaboration?
6. Is collaboration in any way incentivized in your organization?

7. Do I think collaboration is more of a personality trait or influenced by the system?
8. What can I do to encourage a more collaborative climate within my organization?

ORGANIZATION DESIGN

Organization design is a strategic process aimed at harmonizing an organization's systems and structure to enhance its performance. It involves diagnosing issues and misalignments from a holistic systems perspective and striving to optimize organizational effectiveness. The primary objective is to bolster organizational performance by refining its design and operational framework.

1. What is my current organizational structure and how does it affect organizational communications?
2. How did this structure come into being?
3. How is this structure helpful/harmful?
4. If I were going to improve my organizational structure, how would I do it?
5. Does my current structure support cooperation or a silo mentality?
6. How does my organization's current design affect production?
7. Do policies and procedures support mission execution or create inefficiencies?
8. Are people recognized and rewarded for activities that align with mission execution and organizational priorities? Or are rewards and recognition programs misaligned to mission execution?
9. How well does job design support overall organization design?

10. Is reorganization a true/optimal solution or a way to appear to solve a problem?

HUMAN CAPITAL MANAGEMENT

Human Capital Management is the process of soliciting, hiring, onboarding, training, and retaining the workforce. To maximize the levels of employee engagement, motivation, and productivity to enable the organization and the people in it to grow and prosper.

1. What is the current turnover rate within your organization?
2. How can your recruitment, onboarding, and retention processes be enhanced?
3. Is there ample opportunity for career advancement within the organization?
4. How can your training and development initiatives be optimized?
5. How are you preparing your staff for the future?
6. How might your workforce be more productive?
7. How good is your reporting and analytics?
8. How well are you planning for future workforce needs?
9. Do you know the gaps between the future state and current state of operations?

DECISION MAKING/PROBLEM SOLVING

Decision making is the ability to make decisions without hesitation, even when all the information is not known. The ability to act and implement programs and processes. Problem solving is the ability to come up with answers or solutions to current problems and develop a corrective plan of action.

1. I am most decisive when I…
2. I am least decisive when I…
3. How do I typically handle decision making when not everything is known?
4. What decision making criteria do I use in groups/teams?
5. What system, if any, do I use to prioritize my work?
6. How do I develop my solutions?
7. Do my solutions tend to address the immediate situation as well as future concerns?
8. Do I tend to come up with single solutions or several alternatives to problems?
9. What do I do when there is no good solution?

CHAPTER 8

More Wisdom Bits

Terse statements that often have deep meaning and provide an opportunity for discussion and reflection. Rather than merely reading through them as sentences in a book, read each one, pause, think and reflect. This is how you will get the most from this chapter.

1. Most people are as happy as they decide to be.
2. Sustainable change requires both system and behavioral change.
3. Organizational improvement/change is a long-term process, not a short-term event.
4. Why is there never enough time to do it right, but always enough time to do it over?
5. Facts are often interpreted, but interpretations and facts are not the same.
6. Emotions influence how you interpret current events.
7. Be careful of the stories you tell yourself.
8. Your emotions influence your anticipated or imagined future.
9. We tend to exaggerate data to support our statements.
10. If you believe you will get better, you will apply yourself more.
11. Feedback is information only; our interpretation makes it positive or negative.
12. Your attitude toward others says more about you than them.

13. The more judgmental you are, the less time and energy there is for caring.
14. Blaming is usually destructive to the relationship.
15. Avoiding doing something you are not good at means you will never get good at it.
16. People can be changed by the organization and can change the organization.
17. When leadership changes, so does the culture.
18. The more dynamic the group, the better the group dynamics.
19. It is difficult to be something you have never been.
20. Our perceptions, judgments, and paradigms create the world we live in.
21. You can change the organization just by changing yourself.
22. If you are not dealing with the system, then you are not dealing with the organization.
23. There is always a consequence, sometimes social, sometimes natural, sometimes both.
24. You bring yourself with you everywhere.
25. Those that focus on what they don't have are never satisfied, but those that focus on what they do have often are.
26. Your vision of the future comes from your dreams, keep dreaming.
27. Doing something about it is better than talking about it.
28. Some people are so busy making a living they forget to make a life.
29. There are usually more issues than is known.
30. Feedback is a gift that reduces blind spots.
31. You cannot plan everything.

32. By tolerating or enduring the problem, you are helping to continue it.
33. Sustainable organizational change occurs in small increments more often than in large scale change initiatives.
34. It is difficult to lead others when you cannot lead or manage yourself.
35. There are no hopeless situations, you can always do something.
36. Nothing is impossible except saying so.
37. Destiny is not a location, but something you create.
38. We influence change by our influence.
39. Resistance to change is really a drive for sameness.
40. We resist most that which is unknown.
41. There is no such thing as a bad emotion, they are all a rich source of information.
42. The drive for acceptance, to fit in, is what acculturates people to the organization.
43. We tend to only see what we look for.
44. It is difficult to be aware of what you don't know.
45. Many people think they understand before they know.
46. People naturally defend themselves from blame.
47. Employee Engagement is a result, not a program.
48. It is just as important to talk and be heard as it is to listen and be quiet.
49. In an environment of rapid change, there may not be answers, only adaptations.
50. Never let your limitations limit you, after all, they are only limitations until you succeed.

APPENDIX I

Case Chapter – Case Outcomes

This section provides the known outcomes of various cases. While some cases may still be ongoing, the consultant's involvement has ceased, leaving the final outcome uncertain. The presented outcomes, though not always ideal, reflect what transpired. Additionally, when the steps of the process are discernible, they are outlined here for clarity.

CASE #1: THE PRESIDENT

Not all of the senior leaders were supportive of the change initiative, and this violated the eighty percent rule (OD for the Accidental Practitioner, 2022). Additionally, there was internal competition among the senior leaders. Both are major red flags. At the president's insistence, the training was provided to all employees. The training was generally well received and generated both hope and excitement among certain groups which continued with learning more about their own subcultures, systems, and processes. A nice benefit.

The president was asked to step down and take a different position elsewhere and he was the main supporter of this initiative. With the driving force no longer behind the program, the effort was placed on hold by the new director, and never to be brought up again. The internal point of contact decided he could do a better job himself and the entire effort ceased to exist, which is exactly what some of the skeptics said would happen when they took the training.

Two critical factors were violated, one, not having 80% support of the senior leaders, and two, moving too fast away from the senior leaders involving both frontline and mid-level employees when senior leaders themselves were not completely on board. The effort was more of a costly fad than a system changing initiative.

CASE #2: SINCERE ABOUT CHANGE

In the beginning, the relationship between the HR director and the CEO was unknown. It was not until after the training programs were delivered that this information became known to the consultants. The CEO was not the type of person who would even admit that he was doing this just to please the HR director. While the CEO was brought into various conversations, he always seemed ok with the consultant's recommendations, until the price tag got too high and then he put a stop to all activities.

Unfortunately, there was no infrastructure in place to carry on the initial efforts, so everything stopped, and they all went back to their previous equilibrium. This demonstrates the need for transparency and the building of an internal team that can take over the change initiative. Both the CEO and the HR director would have needed to make changes and model those changes to everyone if any change initiative were going to be very successful and sustained. Another well-intended program that turned out to be a fad.

CASE #3: NEW PLANT MANAGER

The number of problems, level of dysfunction, and misalignment were quite high resulting in a never-ending series of day-to-day problems that needed to be addressed with never enough time to strategically plan. The operations manager was an extreme micro-manager, often reversing the new plant manager's decisions without involving him or telling him to the point of even borrowing some of his people to put on a different project without telling him. The operation manager worked eighty-plus hours a week and expected the new plant manager to do the same. Front line and mid-level managers learned to reverse delegate everything to these two individuals, even small decisions like ordering paper towels for the restroom. No consultant was involved in this project. As of the last contact, they have not changed.

CASE #4: DO AS I SAY

After the initial team building programs, where it was discovered that the managers themselves needed to resolve their own conflict and find better ways to cooperate and model to the employees the expected behavior, the consultant gave the senior leaders the feedback. The consultant cited the comments that came from the group, as well as feedback about the abusive supervisor in the hallway, possibly creating a hostile work environment. The senior team accepted the feedback, said thank you and the consultant was never brought back. No further information was available.

CASE #5: TRUST

The senior leaders, like many, were firmly entrenched in their roles and responsibilities. They did not see themselves as the problem, but on occasion saw one another as the problem. Over time, the consultant was able to work with the senior leaders to improve their relationships with each other and to become more collaborative. Being successful translated into an increasing scope of work given to the consultant as he was known to get results (project creep). This distorted his efforts with the senior leaders, and over time, very little fundamentally changed. Ultimately, the consultant left the organization. Shortly after, their operations manager retired, there was a change in leadership, and many more changes were implemented, including the removal of the distrustful director. Ultimately, a change in leadership had to happen before there was a change in roles and responsibilities.

CASE #6: ORGANIZATIONAL DESIGN

Befittingly, the organization decided to pause their reorganization efforts and focus on the immediate problems of high thefts and turnover in two stores, shoplifting and enforcement, and store leadership. Just like training is sometimes used as the cure-all for everything, so is reorganization. Without an improvement in leadership and the systems, any reorganization would likely maintain the same problems and foster new ones. Little else is known about the outcome of this client as once the reorganization was stopped, the organization decided to handle the issues internally.

CASE #7: PETTY CASH

Many of the drivers disliked the dispatcher so they would ask for money, have mixed up receipts, or inaccurate receipts just to annoy and frustrate the dispatcher. It was vindictiveness on the part of the drivers and had nothing to do with the maintenance of the vehicles.

CASE #8: UNAWARE

Jim continued to lose customers and his business was barely hanging on, when he had an unfortunate accident that left him in a wheelchair. Jim found the internal strength to continue on with his business, overcoming his disability and continuing to work as an artist, much to his credit. While able to overcome his physical disability, he was not able to overcome his mental state, continued to be negative, continued to lose customers and eventually went out of business. Listen to your self-talk every day; is it mostly negative or positive? A preponderance of thoughts one way or the other will probably determine what kind of a day you are having and are going to have. The good news is that you can change your attitude anytime you want. You can break an old habit and begin a new one.

CASE #9: HOME SYSTEM

A senior level steering committee was formed to direct this effort. Further, a fact-finding team was formed to discuss the issue and how such a large endeavor would unfold. Representatives from all around the country were invited by regions to ensure geographical and cultural differences. All that is known at the time of this writing was they were working hard to meet a deadline and the specific recommendations are unknown. This was a strategic decision to involve as many senior leaders as possible on both committees, recognizing that this initiative would need a lot of support for years.

CASE #10: DISTANCE FROM HEADQUARTERS

One of the most frequently used approaches to conflict is avoidance, and this situation was no different. Senior leaders avoided known issues for years because they were uncertain on how to proceed. This may or may not have been a wise choice; however, we do know that the longer an issue continues, the harder it is to change and the longer it takes to be resolved. While plans were being made to address the employees' concerns, morale, communication, complaints, and the like, they received a severe budget cut and had to now think about how many people they needed to lay off. Naturally, all the priorities changed, and the consultant was not part of these plans. So, no further information is known as of this writing.

CASE #11: PEOPLE OR SYSTEMS

Due to the intensity of emotions, the hostility of the union representative, and the number of people issues, it was decided to have both venting and team building sessions. After four-to-six months of meetings, the professional staff had resolved most of their differences and were working with others from different divisions, solving their excessive workload issues. Several management changes were made, which also helped. The sharing of other office personnel during peak times not only helped reduce the workload but improved cooperation and attitude among all staff. They were more patient with one another. Additionally, a few of the more contentious people were moved around, which solved the situation at least for the time being. One hated manager took a different position and that also helped to reduce tensions. The very hostile union representative was voted out at the next election, further reducing staff tensions. All in all, this was a very successful change initiative that focused first on the people and then on the system.

CASE #12: LONG MEETING

The solution that was the quickest and most effective was that senior leaders dissolved the entire committee and replaced it with a limited number of people to resolve the issue with a tight deadline.

CASE #13: MERGER MANIA

The time frame is not realistic for a 4,000-to-6,000-person company, especially one with so many problems. The company began tackling as many of the issues that they could handle one after another, and two and half years later, most of them were resolved. It took another year (a total of three and a half years) before you could safely say the companies were fully merged. The company still operates today as a merged company; however, it is significantly smaller and divested of its brick-and-mortar locations. The merger brought forth many issues (as is often the case) not previously considered and the company was forced to deal with them. Their stock price went down and it took them a decade to reemerge with a new sense of purpose and mission.

Case #14: I am Biased

Gloria moved to a different state and continues to work with smaller, more mission-driven companies to her satisfaction and enjoyment. This was her journey to understand what was important to her and the kind of work she liked to do.

APPENDIX II

Gaining Experience

If you are new to the field or in a graduate degree program, you may be curious how you can gain experience in this field so you can start applying your skills. The following list includes suggestions we have for doing so. There are many other opportunities not listed here.

- Pro Bono Work (offer your services free of charge to gain experience)
- Church /religious groups
- Non-Profit organizations
- Village and small city governments
- Townships
- Environmental groups land trusts
- Associations
- Franchise organizations
- Startups, mom & pop organizations
- Family run organizations
- Chamber of Commerce
- Presentations at conferences
- Podcasts
- Special interest groups
- Professional associations
- Advertise your services
- Community organizations
- Online programs

- Publish, articles, blogs
- Job boards
- Career fairs
- Work study programs
- Internships
- Conflict resolution groups/organizations
- Paid work
- Teaching at a community college or university
- Subcontract with a larger consulting firm
- Work with professional associations to get work
- Ask to be placed on projects outside of your current scope of work that expose you to new skills.
- Take a formal detail or temporary role in your organization aligned to your skill development.
- Request to join a mentorship program or formal development program that includes exposure to new work.

BIBLIOGRAPHY

Galbraith Management Consultants LTD. *Star Model*. July 19, 2023.
https://www.jaygalbraith.com/services/star-model.

Goodman, M. *Systems Thinking: What, why, when, where, and how?* July 19, 2023.
https://thesystemsthinker.com/systems-thinking-what-why-when-where-and-how/.

Huitt, W. *Stages of Mastery*. November 5, 2023.
http://www.edpsycinteractive.org/edpsyc/stgmstry.html.

Kilmann Diagnostics. July 30, 2023.
https://kilmanndiagnostics.com/overview-thomas-kilmann-conflict-mode-instrument-tki/.

Kotter, J.P. *Leading Change, With a New Preface by the Author* (1Red.). Harvard Business Review Press, 2012.

McKinsey & Company. *Changing Change Management,* 2015. Accessed October 29, 2023.
https://www.mckinsey.com/featuredinsights/leadership/changing-change-management.

Meadows, Donella H. *Thinking in Systems, A Primer*.
Vermont: Chelsea Greem Publishing, 2008.

Merriam-webster.com, s.v., "knowledgeable." Accessed July 19, 2023.
https://www.merriamwebster.com/dictionary/knowledgable

Merriam-webster.com, s.v., "proactive." Accessed July 19, 2023.
https://www.merriam-webster.com/dictionary/proactive.

Merriam-webster.com, s.v., "reactive." Accessed July 19, 2023.
https://www.merriam-webster.com/dictionary/reactive.

Merriam-webster.com, s.v., "skillful." Accessed July 19, 2023.
https://www.merriam-webster.com/dictionary/skillful.

Platt, J. *The Excitement of Science*. Boston: Houghton Mifflin, 1962.

Popper. K. *The Logic of Scientific Discovery.* New York: Basic Books, 1956.

Taylor, F.W. *The Principles of Scientific Management.* Dover Publications, 1997.

Tuckman, Bruce. *Developmental Sequence in Small Groups*. Group Facilitation: A Research and Applications Journal. 63 (6): 71–72. doi:10.1037/h0022100. PMID 14314073. Archived from the original on 2015-11-29. Retrieved July 29, 2023.

RECOMMENDED READING

Block, Peter. Flawless Consulting: A Guide to Getting Your Expertise Used. Austin, Tex.: Learning Concepts, 1981.

Cummings, Thomas G., and Worley, Christopher G. Organizational Development & Change. 10th ed. Stamford, Conn.: Cengage Learning, 2015.

Grenny, Joseph, Kerry Patterson, Ron McMillan, Al Switzler, and Emily Gregory. Crucial Conversations, Third Edition: Tools for Talking When Stakes are High. New York: McGraw Hill, 2022.

Jamieson, David J., Robert C. Barnett, and Anthony F. Buono. Consultation for Organizational Change Revisited. A Volume in Research in Management Consulting and Contemporary Trends In Organization Development and Change. Charlotte, NC: Information Age Publishing, Inc, 2016.

Jamieson, David J., Allen H. Church, and John D. Vogelsgang. Enacting Values-Based Change: Organization Development in Action. Cham, Switzerland: Palgrave Macmillan, 2018.

Justice, Tom, and David J. Jamieson. The Facilitators Fieldbook. 2nd ed. New York, NY: Amacom, 2012.

Katz, Judith, and Frederick A. Miller. Be Big. Step Up. Step Out. Be Bold. Daring to do our best work together. San Francisco: Berrett-Koehler Publishers, Inc., 2008.

Kotter, J.P. Leading Change, With a New Preface by the Author. 1st ed. Harvard Business Review Press, 2012.

Lencioni, Patrick. The Five Dysfunctions of a Team: A Leadership Fable. San Francisco: Josey-Bass, 2022.

Meadows, Donella H. Thinking in Systems: A Primer. Vermont: Chelsea Green Publishing, 2008.

Miller, Frederick A., Monica E. Biggs, and Judith H. Katz. Change Champions: A Dialogic Approach to Creating an Inclusive Culture. North Vancouver, BC: BMI Publishing, 2022.

Miller, Frederick A., and Judith H. Katz. Safe Enough to Soar: Accelerating Trust, Inclusion & Collaboration in the Workplace. Oakland, CA: Berrett-Koehler Publishers, Inc.

Schein, Edgar, and Peter Schein. Organizational Culture and Leadership. 5th ed. Hoboken, NY: Wiley, 2017.

Schein, Edgar. Process Consultation Revisted: Building the Helping Relationship. Reading, Mass.: Addison Wesley, 1999.

Senge, Peter, C. Otto Scharmer, Joseph Jaworski, and Betty Sue Flowers. Presence: Human Purpose and the Field of the Future. New York: Crown Business, 2004.

Vogelsgang, John, Maya Townsend, Matt Minihan, David Jamieson, Judy Vogel, Annie Vets, Cathy Royal, and Lynne Valek. Handbook for Strategic HR: Best Practices in Organization Development from the OD Network. New York, NY: Amacom, 2012.

AUTHOR BIOGRAPHIES

Larry Kokkelenberg Ph.D.

Dr. Larry Kokkelenberg, author, consultant, trainer, scholar, practitioner. Dr. Kokkelenberg was the Chief of Employee Engagement and directed the Organization Development group for the US Office of Personnel Management and was on the White House Commission for Employee Engagement prior to retirement. He worked with Stephen Covey as one of the 12 senior consultants working with clients large and small and co-authored the 7 Habits of Highly Effective People classroom workbook. He has been researching, designing, developing, and delivering training and consulting programs for forty years. He has personally trained over 200,000 leaders, executives, managers, and supervisory personnel and consulted with over 200 organizations. He has written or contributed to over 40 training programs during the last forty years. He has authored a pamphlet on Adult Education and has coauthored a book on Organization Development as well as numerous articles and an audio tape series on management. He has a Ph.D. in psychology from Union College in Ohio, an MSW from University of Illinois, and a BA from Illinois Benedictine College in Illinois and has been an entrepreneur for over twenty years running several companies.

Regan Miller, M.S.

Regan Miller is a Team Lead at the U.S. Office of Personnel Management's (OPM) Organization Design Division within OPM's HR Solutions, providing human capital management services to public-sector clients nationwide. Regan previously served in the private sector in training and development positions. Across her federal career, she has served in civilian positions within the Department of Army, and the Defense Logistics Agency. This is Regan's second tour with OPM.

Regan has extensive experience in the full scope of operational and strategic human resource management; she has served in two first line supervisor positions, one of which was overseas. Since 2014, Regan has worked in an HR consulting role leading work in Workforce and Succession Planning, Organizational Design, Results-Oriented Performance Culture, and Organization Development. This led her to partner with Federal agencies to improve workforce practices and structures including the Department of Homeland Security, Department of Commerce, Department of Transportation and multiple components of the Department of Labor, among others.

Regan earned a B.S. in Psychology from Salisbury University, and a M.S. in Industrial/Organizational Psychology from the University of Baltimore. Regan is certified in the Organization Culture Inventory (OCI) and Organization Effectiveness Inventory (OEI) from Human Synergistics. Also, Regan is a Certified Professional Coach (CPC) from the College of Executive Coaching.

Companion Book

"This is the book I wish I'd had when I first stumbled into the consulting profession. Read it. Absorb it. Apply it. And pass it on to others." **Dr. Karl Albrecht, Author**

Available Amazon, Barnes & Noble and other retailers.

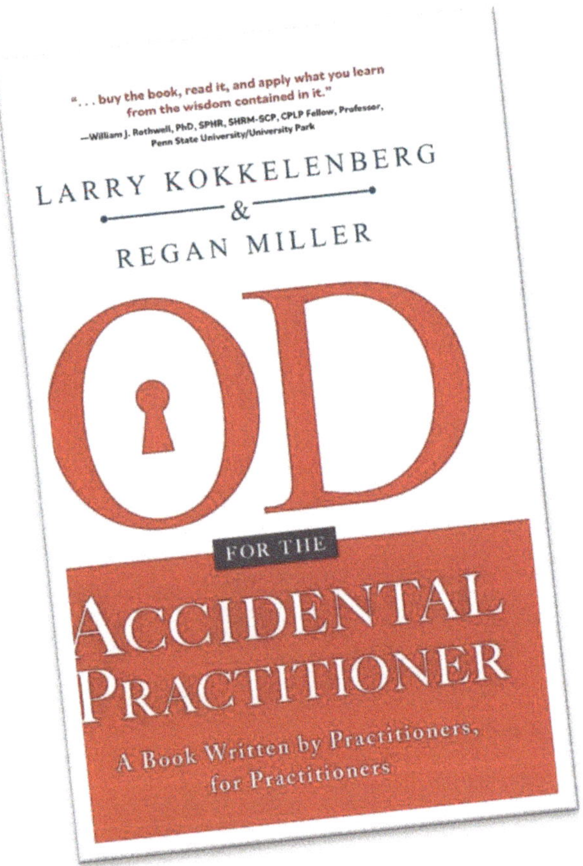